eSPORTS YEARBOOK

Editors: Julia Hiltscher and Tobias M. Scholz
Layout: Tobias M. Scholz
Cover: Photo: P.Strack, ESL
Copyright © 2017 by eSports Yearbook and the Authors of the Articles or Pictures.
ISBN 978-3-7448-0071-6
Production and Publishing House: BoD - Books on Demand, Norderstedt.
Printed in Germany 2017
www.esportsyearbook.com

eSports Yearbook 2015/16

Editors: Julia Hiltscher and Tobias M. Scholz

Contributors:
Viktor Barie, Ho Kai Sze Brenda, Isaque Renovato de Araujo, Fernando Porfírio Soares de Oliveira, Rolf Drenthe, Filbert Goetomo, Christian Esteban Martín Luján, Marc-Andre Messier, Patrick Strack

Content

Preface

By Julia Hiltscher and Tobias M. Scholz

You seem to hear it every year: eSports is growing and can be described as a global phenomenon. We are yet once more stunned by events such as Amazon's purchase of Twitch for nearly 1 billion dollars.

However, the recent year had also revealed the fragility of eSports and furthermore, how adaptable eSports needs to be. One of the authors recently visited South Korea and was stoked to talk about eSports in the "homeland", but only couple of weeks before the trip, the Starcraft 2 league was shut down and several Starcraft 2 teams ceased to exist.

Despite the struggle of Starcraft 2 in South Korea and the cannibalization effects with Starcraft: Brood War, this was nevertheless shocking. Obviously, there was an urge to talk about this drastic development, especially as eSports in Korea definitely was established a sport in the more mainstream sense of the term. Many "Westerners" crave eSports to have such a status in their countries. At least in many Western eSports communities, maybe there are no eSports TV channels but the sport is filling stadiums (e.g. with ESL in the Commerzbank Arena).

Up to that moment, there was nothing but growth in Korea and it seemed that the sky was the limit. It was the first massive setback in the recent months and years.

It seems reasonable to shut down the league, as the business model in South Korea is not that viable as compared to the U.S. or Europe. Money is still being generated mainly by sponsors, whereas the Swedish company MTG (Turtle Entertainment and Dreamhack) is not as dependent on sponsors; and neither is the prime example Fnatic, which remain highly profitable besides the money generated from their sponsors.

So, in talking about the impact of eSports and the recent development, there was a marketing manager from a big Korean game development company who said the following striking sentence: "eSports is dead" (at least in South Korea). And from the experiences in those days, it seems that eSports is currently dying in South Korea. the recent development with Starcraft 2 was, already, pinpointing to the concept that South Korea is no longer the leading eSports country. Sure, the best players are South Korean, but many players moved to non-Korean organizations (e.g. Polt, Jaedong and so on). Although, that is not entirely true for many games, but it was the case for Starcraft 2.

Analyzing the case revealed one thing that may be seen as a warning signal: South Korea was highly dominated by traditional companies and, furthermore, organized in a more traditional and top-down way. There was a strong dependence on those companies and no viable business model for any organization within South Korea. However, eSports grew and gained its momentum through new concepts, by being innovative and following new ways. Especially in Europe and the U.S. eSports never followed the rules and did their own thing, be it the streaming idea and abandoning traditional television or the recent intentions of Riot to create their own Internet backbone. That is the driving force behind eSports, though however, recent acquisitions from companies like Amazon or MTG as well as sports teams like Schalke 04 or Philadelphia 76ers are changing the eSports sphere. There may be the tendency for those companies to want to form eSports in a more traditional way. The case of South Korea should be a warning signal, that the traditional way may not be the right way for eSports, in general. From a scientific perspective, the next years will be interesting.

However, on the plus side, eSports is increasingly observed by the sciences and, therefore, we are quite happy to present this new book with a heavy focus on scientific papers about eSports. These papers are revealing of the difference of eSports and state that it is relevant to look at eSports individually. Therefore we are quite happy about the great articles contributed by authors from many different countries and we hope you have a great time reading them.

Yours,

Julia Hiltscher (Christophers)
&
Tobias M. Scholz

… keep on gaming!

Julia Hiltscher was born in 1983 in Westerstede, Germany. She established eMAG – an online eSports magazine – with Tobias Scholz in 2004. She has been a working student at the Electronic Sports League (Turtle Entertainment GmbH) since Feb. 2006, achieved her Master of Arts degree in International Comparative Literature and Media, English and German at Bonn University in June 2009 and has been working at ESL since. As Vice Director Community Management she has helped to create and run lots of successful tournaments such as the Go4 series, IEM or ENC. She can be contacted at: julia.hiltscher@googlemail.com

Tobias M. Scholz is currently holding a position as a Post-Doctoral Researcher at the University of Siegen. After graduating from universities in Germany and the U.S., he has worked as a research and teaching assistant. His field of research is human resource management and organizational behavior.

Spectating the Rift: A Study into eSports Spectatorship

By Ho Kai Sze Brenda

The steady drone of noise by the crowd of some 13,000 people rose into a roar, as players from both teams were grandly elevated into the arena, accompanied by spectacular stage effects and stylish introductory videos. Bright lights were trained on the players, and their every movement was captured on camera- to be broadcasted to some 32 million viewers worldwide via online streaming and TV stations. This was how it was like at the League of Legends (LoL) Season 3 World Championship Finals in 2013- a groundbreaking event that became the most watched eSports event in history.

eSports, an abbreviation for 'electronic sports', has experienced a phenomenal explosion in popularity in recent years. To the uninvolved, the term 'eSports' may remain an unfamiliar one- in layman's terms, it refers to competitive professional video gaming, and is an equivalent to other terms such as cyber-athleticism or professional gaming (pro-gaming). The popularity of eSports today is visible in many ways. For one, prize monies for eSports tournaments have reached an all-time high- statistics report a 350% jump from year 2010 to the 25 million USD awarded in 2013. (Barberie & Llamas 2014) On top of that, viewership of such tournaments has shot through the roof, reaching more than 71 million viewers worldwide in year 2013 alone (Barberie & Llamas 2014), making it more of a spectator sport than ever. On top of that, in 2013, U.S. authorities made the move to recognise eSports pro gamers as professional athletes, granting them visas to enter the U.S. for events under that identifier. (Tassi 2013)

Such immense popularity and recognition makes it clear that eSports is a phenomenon that cannot simply be ignored, or swept under the rug as an extension of video gaming- but instead brings forth a need for academic attention onto itself. Although eSports has received some attention and is increasingly being studied in academia, there remains a lack of research into the spectatorship of eSports- as at first glance, eSports is seemingly about competitive gamers and tournaments, those taking direct action upon the game, resulting in skepticism as well as a general overlooking and lack of recognition of the importance of spectatorship. (Ditsmarch 2013; Taylor 2012) As such, the bulk of available research on eSports has been dedicated towards the direct participants partaking it in (i.e. pro gamers) (Mora & Heas 2005; Reeves et al. 2009; Witkowski 2012) the debate over whether eSports is a sport (Hutchins 2008; Johansson & Thiborg 2011; Witkowski 2009; 2012), or the technologies and interfaces related to eSports (Kow & Young 2013; Rambusch, Jakobsson & Pargman 2007). There have been calls for further empirical research into the cultural aspects of eSports, such as that by Seo (2013) who called for further research into the eSports experience, and Ditsmarch (2013) who called for qualitative research consulting eSports spectators.

Taylor (2012) argued that spectatorship plays a key role in the eSports scene, and that spectators are the driving force behind eSports:

"fans do not simply consume but are crucial participants in the production of cultural products… they infuse energy into events, giving meaning and social importance to activities… and often provide important contributions through their participation in various media (on-line or off)." (Taylor 2012, p.188)

This is especially in light of the shift in consumer participation- from the more passive audiences of the past to the more active, participative culture evident in audiences today. (Jenkins 2006, p.3) Games have always been termed a 'co creative' media, where neither developers nor player creators are solely respon-sible for the production of the final assemblage that is 'the game', requiring input from both (Morris cited in Kennedy & Dovey 2006 p. 123)- The same can be said for eSports, that the 'final assemblage' of the eSports experience is co-created, by spectators, the game company and other stakeholders. The eSports experience is valuable in the experience economy of today, where increasingly, companies have to stage experiences that will engage consumers and connect with them in a personal and memorable way in order to generate economic value. (Pine & Gilmore 1998; 2013)

By conducting a case study on the Oceanic League of Legends eSports scene, I aim to explore ethno-graphically the various ways eSports spectators participate, the new meanings and identities that emerge from such participation, and how these processes format to become an essential part of the overall 'eS-ports experience', from which eSports game companies profit.

There are many ways to carry out audience research- I chose to focus on the social networks and activi-ties within the Oceanic eSports gaming community, studying the ways eSports spectators develop and maintain social interactions with other spectators, the game company, and various symbolic values that emerge from such social exchanges.

The research fieldwork was undertaken during the period of October 2014- April 2015, during which I conducted participation-observation at two eSports events- League of Legends at PAX AUS 2014, and fan-organised event MOG MOBAR- and through my continued participation with the Oceanic eSports community. During this period, I also interviewed 11 LoL eSports spectators on their experiences with eSports.

Literature Review

The Terminology of 'eSports'

eSports, which stands for 'electronic sports', is a term commonly used to refer to competitive professio-nal video gaming. There are various other equivalent terms for this activity as well- such as cyber-athle-ticism or professional gaming (pro-gaming); yet there was no scientific or academic definition available, until 2006, when Wagner (2006) adapted the definition of 'sport' by sports scientist Tiedemann into one suitable for eSports, resulting in the definition of eSports as:

"an area of sport activities in which people develop and train mental or physical abilities in the use of information and communication technologies" (Wagner 2006, p. 3) .

Although this definition remains somewhat usable for our purposes, I concur with Ditsmarch (2013) that there are a few aspects missing- the fact that eSports is competitive, and performed through video games. As such, I will be borrowing the slightly altered definition proffered by Ditsmarch (2013) to provide a more precise understanding of eSports in this thesis:

"an area of sport activities in which people develop, train and compare mental or physical abilities using information and communication technologies through video games" (Ditsmarch 2013, p. 4).

One of the most prominent battlefields of early scholarship in eSports stems from a disarmingly straight-forward question- is eSports a sport? After all, much like sports, eSports has several titles that are relatively professionalised- with teams competing for millions of dollars, seasons, playoffs and championship rounds, professional players- 'athletes'- who game for a living, and viewership besting popular sports tournaments such as the NBA Finals and the BCS National Championship. (Super Data Research cited in Schwartz 2014) That is on top of the move in 2013 by the U.S., recognising eSports pro gamers as professional athletes and granting them visas to enter the U.S. for events under that identifier. (Tassi 2013)

What then, stands between eSports from being recognised as a sport?

There are many areas of contention when it comes to the recognition of eSports as sport- namely, the traditional definitions of sport, physicality, phenomenological experience, and the use of technology. Various researchers have contributed to addressing these issues- overall, it was found that although eSports does fulfill the definitional criterions of traditional sport (Jonasson & Thiborg 2010; Witkowski 2009; 2012), has considerable physical demands (Ferrari 2013; Witkowski 2012), has a phenomenological experience perceivably in line with sporting sensations (Witkowski 2009), technological (computing) aspects akin to that of sporting technologies (Taylor 2012; Witkowski 2012) it remains that sport cannot be recognised simply by such definitional criterions or comparisons.

Wagner (2006) raises that "the activities we will accept as sport disciplines will change as our value system change" (Wagner 2006, p. 2), bringing up the issue that sport is a social construct, more than anything else. This is supported by Kutte Jönsson (2007), who asserts that sport is what the sports 'world' considers as sport. (Jönsson cited in Jonasson & Thiborg 2010)

As such, eSports would require social recognition from stakeholders such as the sports community in order to be considered a sport, which at this point has largely yet to be achieved. Therefore, for now, eSports is best left to be considered a discipline of its own, to be studied and developed unconstrained by the stranglehold of the term Sport. As put by Hutchins (2008), eSports cannot be thought in terms of media or sport or computer gaming, as to do so would be misreading the subject matter and ignoring the distinctive feature of eSports, which is not shared by traditional sport- "the material interpenetration of media content, sport, and networked computing." (Hutchins 2008, p. 863) After all, a traditional sporting game may take place with or without a media platform present, whereas eSports spectatorship will always be mediated via a video interface, even if at a live event.

Participatory Culture, Co-Creation and the eSports Spectator

Who are the eSports spectators, and how do they participate? According to Cheung & Huang (2011), spectators are:

"people who follow the in-game experience, but are not direct participants in the game" (Cheung & Huang 2011, p. 2).

This by no means refers only to spectators completely engrossed in the experience (like that of a focused moviegoer in the theatre); people may simply be casual spectators, multi-tasking watching an eSports game with other activities such as perusing social media, or socialising with friends.

A useful way of understanding the nature of spectatorship would be to look at game ludology, which presents the concept of the 'magic circle'. The 'magic circle' is essentially an imaginary space in which play occurs; so the question that is begged here is, is there any place for the spectator within the 'magic circle' of play? (Salen & Zimmerman 2004)

Cheung & Huang (2011) succinctly summarise the position of the spectator in the 'magic circle'- basically, a spectator is considered to be in the magic circle if they are committed to in-game values, are invested in the tension of play, and share a vicarious relationship with the player. It is indeed possible for a spectator to be outside the 'magic circle'- by lacking understanding or interest in the game, or simply refusing to adopt the game values.

This shows us that spectatorship can indeed be a component of the entire concept of play as we understand it. This is especially true of eSports, where spectators tend to be a "player/spectator hybrid" (Ditsmarch 2013, p.21), most eSports spectators often being players of the game they spectate.

Spectator participation and projects are characteristic of a flourishing eSports scene. Scholz (2011) raises this point in context of the StarCraft broadcasting scene, bringing up three forms of participation by viewers:
1. the BarCraft movement- events where spectators gather in public settings to view StarCraft tournaments together-,
2. the existence of and interaction within communities,
3. and journalistic coverage done by members of the community.

These forms of participation indeed exemplify the key role that spectators take in constructing the eSports spectatorship experience. In my case study of LoL spectatorship, I will be analysing such forms of participation.

Participatory Culture

In 2006, Yochai Benkler noted that the advanced economies in the world were shifting away from the industrial information economy of the past, towards one of a networked information economy. He characterised this emerging networked information economy as one of decentralized individual action, in which new and important cooperative and coordinate action carried out through radically distributed, nonmarket mechanisms that do not depend on proprietary strategies play a much greater role than before. (Benkler 2006)

That same year, media scholar Henry Jenkins introduced to us the concept at the root of our media system today- convergence. Convergence is characterised as:

> "the flow of content across multiple media platforms, the cooperation between multiple media industries, and the migratory behavior of media audiences who will go almost anywhere in search of the kinds of entertainment experiences they want." (Jenkins 2006, p. 2)

These two concepts demonstrate the economic and cultural logics shaping our media landscape today-the landscape from which eSports spectatorship has developed. As pointed out by Jin (2010):

> "As online gaming has merged with IT, which is essential for the growth of the online game industry, eSports has become a key domain in the digital economy. In fact, eSports has several meanings, and it is important to understand eSports as the convergence of the electronic games, sports, and media" (Jin 2010, p. 61).

Both Jenkins (2006) and Benkler (2006) are careful to note that technology is not the core of their concepts. Benkler (2006) believes that technological determinism in the strict sense (whereby if you have technology, you should expect social structure or relation to emerge) to be false. Likewise, Jenkins (2006) asserts that convergence is more than just a technological shift, considering it a cultural shift where "consumers are encouraged to seek out new information and make connections among dispersed media content." (Jenkins 2006, p. 3)

It is this emphasis upon the cultural and social role of the eSports spectator that is the core understanding of this study. As Ludvigsen & Veersawmy (2010) noted, sports spectators, more than just being a frame for the event, participate in a highly social, active, and self-representational experience of 'spectatoring' revolving around the sport itself.

Besides that, audiences can often play a role in the production of meaning in culture- by reinterpreting and/or modifying objects sold to them, thus taking an active role as producers of other goods. (Crawford 2004)

Central to the participatory culture claim is that the public is seen not as passive consumers of pre-constructed messages, but people who are shaping, sharing, reframing and remixing media content as never before. (Jenkins et al. 2013, p. 2) Produsage is one form of this- content production by consumers, which involves collaborative and continuous building and extending of existing content to further improve it. (Bruns 2006, p.2) Produsage is prevalent in the gaming industry, where user-led innovation and content production in games is commonplace. One prominent example of produsage is the creation of popular first-person shooter (FPS) game Counter-Strike, which started off as a modification of Half-Life, the collective effort of a team of highly-skilled and focused game enthusiasts. But produsage is but one of the many forms of participatory culture. Jenkins et al. (2013) reminds us not to push DIY media making as the be-all and end-all of participatory culture, as that would be overlooking the significance of other kinds of participation- such as the evaluation, appraisal, critique and recirculation of material. Audience activities requiring greater media production skills (e.g. freeware creation) are by no means necessarily more valuable and meaningful to other audience members or to cultural producers than acts of debate or collective interpretation. (Jenkins 2013)

Put succinctly, participatory culture is a culture with:

> "relatively low barriers to artistic expression and civic engagement, strong support for creating and sharing creations, and some type of informal membership whereby experienced participants pass along knowledge to novices… members also believe their contributions matter and feel some degree of social connection with one another" (Jenkins et al. 2009, p. xi).

Some forms of participation include:

- affiliation- memberships in online communities centred around various media
- expressions- producing creative products such as fan videos
- collaborative problem-solving- working together in teams to complete tasks and develop new knowledge
- circulations- shaping the flow of media content (Jenkins et al. 2009)

In my study of Oceanic LoL eSports, I found all four forms of participation to be prevalent in the various roles undertaken by spectators.

It is this active participative role of spectators and its significance that is exactly what I aim to explore and outline in this study on the eSports spectator. Spectators, when taking on active roles, can impact the overall eSports experience, and also shape their own experience with eSports.

Co-Creation

Co-creation is not new to the gaming industry. In 2003, games theorist Sue Morris termed FPS games a 'co creative media', where "neither developers nor players can be solely responsible for production of the final assemblage regarded as 'the game', it requires input from both." (Morris 2003, cited in Dovey & Kennedy 2006, p. 123) Moving away from a purely produsage-centred viewpoint, John Banks (2013) states "co-creativity occurs when consumers contribute a non-trival component of the design, development, production, marketing and distribution of a new or existing product." (Banks 2013, p. 1) This definition is less limiting considering the range of participative activities that can potentially contribute substantially to the 'final assemblage' of the co-creative media. We cannot simply overlook the potential for non-produsage participatory activities to contribute in a non-trivial manner to the end product. This thesis aims to outline the various participatory activities undertaken by eSports spectators, and look into the contribution of these activities.

However, co-creativity remains a problematic concept- if media users are putting in effort to engage and contribute to the 'final assemblage' of co-creative media, aren't we working for free and yet generating value for the media organisations? Aren't corporations exploiting us, by having us provide them with free (unpaid) labour? That seems to be the case, from the viewpoint of an industrial media economy; where co-creativity is seen as a way in which capital extracts surplus value and increases profitability by reducing costs and displacing labour. (Banks & Humphreys 2008, p. 402) Yet, co-creativity should not simply be dismissed with an understanding from the viewpoint of an industrial media economy.

For one, whilst co-creation processes require people to be willing to give up their time and commit themselves to the cause, it is a trade-off, as organisations too, have to be willing to pass over some of their power to participants. (Ind et al. 2012, p. 15) This power comes in the form of letting the product cease to be an entity purely under the control of the organisation, but to be a fluid, moving space of dialogue between the organisation and the stakeholders in the co-creative process. (Ind et al. 2012)

Additionally, free labour is understood as exploitation due to the lack of monetary reward when producing value for the organisation- however, this disregards that rewards can come in other forms besides extrinsic monetary value. Research shows that the dominant motivation for people to take part in co-creative processes is actually intrinsic- for the benefits of learning, meaning making, and as a socialising activity enjoyable for the potential of sharing. (Ind et al. 2012, p. 156) In their case analysis research on modding, Roig et al. (2013) found that modders repeatedly showed commitment to creation of free content, rejected monetization, and stressed their wish to gain some sort of recognition for their contribution to the value of the company, (Roig et al. 2013) revealing that extrinsic monetary compensation is not necessarily a source of motivation. Extrinsic incentives can take second priority, as a secondary feature in helping people rationalise participation.

Yet, it is not generalisable that all who participate in co-creative processes are and will always remain motivated by purely intrinsic rewards. This issue has been raised by Banks & Potts (2010) who found that co-creation has often been approached from the polarized perspectives of either a cultural approach where participants are motivated by a shared communal purpose (such as provision of freeware), or a commercial approach where participants' motivations would be to get a profit (money or job). (Banks & Potts cited in Roig et al. 2013, p. 641)

As Banks (2013) found in his consultancy ethnographic research on co-creativity management at an Australia-based game company, fans often have no singular position on such issues. Some participants were motivated by shared passion for the product, some by satisfaction of their craft, some by social status gained within the community, some by pathways into paid employment, and some by commercial opportunities. On top of that, fan motivations are not static, but dynamic and subject to change- cases of initial non-market and non-financial motivations developing into commercial motivations are not uncommon in the games industry.

This shows that co-creativity is a complex, dynamic process that cannot simply be understood by the polar viewpoints of an industrial or social economy- it would be better understood as an intersection of both enterprise and social networks. As such, Banks & Potts (2010) developed an alternate model of consumer co-creation- the co-evolutionary model, which proposes both cultural factors (identity conceptions, received practices, power relations) and economic factors (implicit contracts, incentives, markets and business models) to affect outcomes of the other, thus shifting away from a one-sided study of single viewpoint, to the study of interaction between the two domains. Interestingly, some key ideas that Banks & Potts (2010) raise in their model (based on the concepts of multiple games theory and theory of social network markets) is that of how consumers often resolve multiple contexts of action (such as intellectual property production, cultural identity, community norms, etc.) into one seamless dynamic context and arrive at a single action identified with in all contexts, and also that consumer co-creation emerges most powerfully in a social network market context- where agents break away from the market function of price as a coordinating factor, instead using social connections and recommendations, access and attention as the coordinating factors (Banks & Potts 2010) .

It is important for us to study co-creation, as mentioned by Banks & Humphreys (2008):

> "user-led labour, in all its uncertainty, is an agent of change that unsettles existent industrial knowledge regimes. The changes wrought by shifting the contributions of users toward the core of commercial business models may well result in open innovation structures and change our understanding of what markets are." (Banks & Humphreys 2008, p. 416)

There are various implications in such changes, such as the destruction of professional (paid) labour, or the perspectives we should consider in attempting to manage such changes. This thesis aims to contribute to such discourse via our own study on co-creative practices and its nuances in the emergent eSports industry.

Another study on co-creativity that can inform my study into eSports would be Yuri Seo (2013)'s study into value co-creation in eSports. Seo's research reveals that the experience of eSports is co-created by multiple marketing actors- gaming companies, players, online communities, governing bodies, and other stakeholders- who play a part in enriching and sustaining the experiential value of eSports; thus leading Seo to argue that the market should not be perceived as simply hosts-and-guests of eSports, but as a constellation of marketing actors participating in the co-creation of value. (Seo 2013, p. 1543) This is not dissimilar to what I aim to argue in my thesis, as through my own methods, I am exploring specifically the role that spectators play, amongst the 'constellation of marketing actors participating in the co-creation of value'.

Affective and Embodied Experience

But how is the experience perceived by the spectator himself/ herself?

Taylor (2012) noted the importance of addressing affective and embodied aspects of spectatorship, and brought up her observation that:

> "spectators can become activated in their bodies, sitting forward in anticipation during a tense moment, intently focused on the screen, feeling the visceral reverberations of the digital action within their bodies, cheering with excitement or clapping when victory happens." (Taylor 2012, p. 186)

Similarly, in Taylor & Witkowski's (2010) participation-observation at a Mega-LAN event, they observed that:

> "simply watching a familiar game connects you, somehow viscerally, to your own embodied experience of play... can reactivate one's own sense of, and desire for, play. It can reground your identity as a gamer and even viscerally pull you into that play moment, sometimes even transforming it into a kind of shared experience." (Taylor & Witkowski 2010, p. 197)

These observations certainly point towards how the affective and embodied experiences of spectating can be significant- not only in creating a memorable experience (that may be shared with others at the scene), but also in reconnecting one with the game being spectated.

Cheung & Huang (2011) have noted some related aspects of spectatorship in their study of StarCraft spectators- they developed three key themes: the Spectator Ecosystem, Circles of watching, and Co-Labouring in Spectatorship. The Spectator Ecosystem posits that there are interrelated ties between fellow spectators and players- these ties leading to shared emotional experiences and the establishment of social norms (players promise not to disappoint fans, spectators judge players according to understanding of sportsmanship and 'bad-mannered' play). The Circle of watching refers to how other participants (besides the gamers themselves) engage in performative behaviour- such as the crowd engaging in little performances such as commentating the match themselves, hyping up their peers, and other reactionary performances. Co-labouring in spectatorship basically refers to how spectators work together to produce an enjoyable spectating experience; commentators labour to shape the experience, members of the crowd find narratives to latch onto, people sharing information throughout (Cheung & Huang 2011).

These are themes that have not been ignored in research on traditional sporting events. For one, Ludvigsen & Veersawmy (2010) who studied the active spectator experience at sporting events, found spectating to be a sports-like activity in itself, and that the sporting event may be a frame for social experiences that are lived, remembered and felt. (Ludvigsen & Veersawmy 2010; Fairley cited in Ludvigsen & Veersawmy 2010) They posit that whilst spectator experiences are often thought of as merely events and interactions that occur during the game itself, arguably, the spectator experience unfolds in broader spatial and temporal context- spectators actively engage in and co-create their collective experience, through various participatory practices (self-presentation, activities, fan-culture, identification), that may occur even before or after the event (Ludvigsen & Veersawmy 2010).

In this study, I will examine such themes and aspects of spectatorship, in the context of eSports spectatorship.

Experience Economy

What then, is the role of the game company in relation to all this? The concept of the experience economy was first brought up by Pine & Gilmore (1998) where they posited an economic shift from the service economy to an experience economy. This fundamental shift in the fabric of the global economy holds the implication that companies now have to stage experiences that will engage customers and connect with them in a personal and memorable way, in order to generate economic value. (Pine & Gilmore 1999; 2013)

Creative industries, consisting of sectors that serve consumer demands where the aesthetic or symbolic value is higher than the use value, are often considered as the core of the experience economy. (Vang & Tschang 2013) Therefore, it comes as no surprise that the videogames industry- amongst others such as theatre and film- became one of the oft-cited examples of the experience economy, as successful games tend to provide a fully designed experience for its consumers. (Vang & Tschang 2013, p. 405) It can be said that eSports came as a natural extension to this already experience-centred industry- in their study of the historical development of eSports, Borowy & Jin (2013) identified eSports to be a hallmark of the experience economy, and a succession of consumer practices whose development was coterminous with the rise of event marketing as a leading promotional business strategy.

Notably, Seo (2013) in his study of marketing landscape of eSports in relation to the experience economy, offered a holistic perspective to the experiential value derived from eSports, according to 'The Four Realms of Experience' (4Es) model developed by Pine & Gilmore (1988). He detailed the variety of activities, and thus experiences, that can occur throughout eSports consumption- for example, the use of Internet cafes as a social space for the Escapist experience, the immersion of spectators and players in eSports tournaments as an Esthetic experience- thus creating experiential value in their own ways. Additionally, Seo (2013) posits the eSports experience as one not produced by computer-game designers and transmitted to consumers, but co-created by multiple marketing actors- within which are our eSports spectators. This goes to show that indeed, spectators play a part in creating the experiential value for eSports, which can be translated into economic value for the eSports game.

After all, as Sundbo & Sørensen (2013) note, experience can be considered part of marketing activities, as it increases attention to the product and consumer loyalty.

The value of eSports is not something that has gone unnoticed by game companies, as it has been found that eSports is considered a key marketing vehicle and revenue driver for online game publishers, with companies such as Riot Games, Wargaming, Valve and Ubisoft emphasizing eSports in their marketing strategies (Llamas & Barberie 2014) .

Bringing it all together, in this experience economy, experiences in eSports can be considered to be "formal economic activities that have the aim to deliver elements that can provoke experiences in people who pay directly or indirectly for them." (Sundbo & Sørensen 2013, p. 5) The experiential value of eSports has the potential and ability to generate economic value not only for gaming companies, but also for companies looking to reach out to the same target audiences. This study looks into how experiential value co-created by spectators in the eSports scene is capitalised upon, to create economic value for the game company.

Methodology

Research Questions

With the consideration of how eSports spectators might be playing a key role in the phenomenal popularity of the eSports industry, the profileration of participatory culture and co-creation in media consumption, and the resulting debate on the capitalisation of such activity, I developed my following line of questioning:

How do eSports spectators participate and make sense of their own eSports experience, how this participation contributes to co-creating the overall 'eSports experience', and what is the resulting value for the eSports game company?

Design of the Study

This thesis makes use of qualitative ethnographic research methods- namely, participation-observation and semi-structured interviews.

The choice of ethnographic methods is due to the nature of this study – in looking at spectatorship, we're looking at audiences and their cultural behaviour. This makes ethnography the best fit, being focused on human society, and culture – the beliefs, values, attitudes that structure the behaviour patterns of a specific group of people -, and often used in media studies to draw out broader contexts surrounding media usage and engagement.

Going into specifics, I chose the methods of both participation-observation and semi-structured interviews- both complementary methods as participation-observation is a technique concerned with "what people actually do than what they say they do", (Brennan 2013, p. 160) whereas semi-structured interviewing is based on what people say they do.

The Case: League of Legends Oceania, Sample Selection and Data Collection

The eSports game that this thesis focuses on is League of Legends (LoL), developed by American video game publisher Riot Games.

League of Legends is a MOBA (multiplayer online battle arena) game that involves two teams of (usually, depending on game mode and map) five players working together to battle the other team with the objective of destroying the opponent team's base (the Nexus).

The basis for selection is simple – LoL is arguably the most popular eSports title at this point of time, with an immense number of people playing and spectating. Riot Games reports a total of 67 million players per month, and 27 million daily players. (Riot 2015) As for spectators, just for League of Legends Worlds Championship Series 2014, the annual and most popular tournament of the game, there was a reported 27 million unique viewer count for the finals alone, and 179 million hours of the entire LoL Worlds Championship season watched online across the world (Riot 2014).

Notably, LoL, as with many other games, consists of multiple servers accommodating different regions – both for technical (issues of high latency) and cultural purposes (such as language differences).

For this thesis, I bound my study to a specific region – for reasons of accessibility as well as limitations to the scale of research possible for this thesis – therefore using only participants from the Oceanic region.

League of Legends Oceania (LoL OCE) is a fairly new server, launched in 28 June 2013, catering to people residing in the Oceanic region. The eSports scene in Oceania is relatively less developed than that of major LoL regions such as North America, Europe, Korea, China and Southeast Asia, although Oceania does have its own league, the Oceanic Pro League. (Riot Mirhi 2014) The LoL OCE eSports scene makes for an interesting study as it is still in a dynamic process of development, as compared to the more established major LoL leagues.

Sample Selection and Data Collection

Throughout this study, I made use of purposive sampling. I chose to make use of two eSports events as the sites from which I would carry out participation-observation at, as well as recruit participants for my interviews. These two eSports events were:

1. MOG MOBAR 2014 – LoL World Championships (Grand Finals)

Photograph 1: MOG MOBAR 2014 seating area

Held on the 19th October 2014, MOG MOBAR is a viewing event for the LoL World Championships (Grand Finals), held by eSports fan-made organisation Ministry of Gaming. Held at a bar (Lagerfield) at Crown Casino Melbourne, this is a paid-entry event where eSports fans gather to watch the finals together, and participate in the various activities organised (e.g. cosplayer showcase, pub quiz, raffle. Notably, this event is fan-organised.

2. PAX AUS 2014 (Penny Arcade eXpo Australia)

Photograph 2: League of Legends at PAX AUS 2014

PAX Australia 2014 is a large-scale annual gaming festival, held 31st October- 2nd November 2014. I chose this event as Riot Games was making an appearance with League of Legends – they occupied a huge area in the exhibition hall, with a stage and seating area, at which they held the LoL Oceanic Season 3 tournament finals live.

Besides my participation-observation at the events itself, I also took notes from my continued participation with the Oceanic eSports community, useful in providing insight beyond the selected events.

My interviewee recruitment was also not limited to the above events, as I chose to make use of snowball sampling (asking for referrals from recruited interviewees).

All in all, this resulted in 11 LoL spectators (8 males, 3 females) who participated in the interviews. The participants mainly reside in Australia, with the exception of two residing in New Zealand. Participation was voluntary, with no incentive offered. Interviews were conducted at the participants' convenience, either face-to-face or via Skype audio call. Interviews began with questions asking about their game and eSports consumption, before moving into experiences, participation and thoughts on the topic, pursuing relevant lines of questioning.

Data Analysis

Ethnographic data analysis is more than description – it is a combination of description, analysis and interpretation. (Merriam 2013) In this case study, I seek to provide "an intensive, holistic description and analysis of a single, bounded unit", (Merriam 2013, p. 203) in overall a holistic, detailed ethnographic account of my exploration into the Oceanic eSports scene.

Case Study

An ecosystem of eSports spectatorship

Prior to attending an eSports event or spectating eSports online, one might be under the impression that the experience is one provided solely by the game company.

However, going in with a lens geared towards observing what the building blocks of the eSports spectator experience might be, I observed an ecosystem by which the spectators work together (along with the game company and other stakeholders) to contribute to the eSports experience.

For easy reference, I developed a diagram of the spectators' participatory roles within the ecosystem:

Diagram 1: Model of Spectator Participatory Ecosystem

As seen in the diagram, I identified the various roles eSports spectators step into during their participation. The term ecosystem is key to this diagram – much like how Cheung & Huang (2011) used the word 'ecosystem' in their study of the StarCraft spectator, where they recognised the interrelated ties between spectators and gamers, I use the word ecosystem when referring to the participative relationships that occur, because many of these roles undertaken (and thus activities carried out) would not be able to sustain or be meaningful without their fellow participants. Additionally, a healthy ecosystem of participation would also lead to an enhanced eSports experience.

It's important to note that these roles are not mutually exclusive- for example, a pro-gamer (not in-game at that moment) may turn into a focused spectator at an event, or a streamer at home. Additionally, this diagram is in no way exhaustive, as spectators constantly find new ways to participate, and as more affordances that aid them in doing so emerge- however this is useful as a basic overview of the current participatory ecosystem of the Oceanic eSports scene. Following this, I will provide a brief elaboration of the roles identified in the ecosystem:

Competitive Gamer

Photograph 3: Oceanic eSports team competing at PAX AUS 2014

The most prominent participatory activity in the ecosystem- without them, there would be no tournaments nor eSports. Besides their direct participation in tournaments, they also slip into this role when making event appearances or fan-interaction activities.

During MOG MOBAR, members of the Oceanic team 'The Chiefs' were clearly identifiable from their blue 'CHIEFS' team jackets. They were invited to the MOBAR not just to watch the Worlds Finals, but also to go onstage for an interview and Q&A session, and later to participate in 2v2 LoL games against members of the public at the LAN gaming area. It was the same for PAX, where teams not only participated by competing onstage during the Oceanic Pro League (OPL), but also participated in fan-signs autographing LoL posters.

Photograph 4: Members of Oceanic team 'The Chiefs' onstage (with event host) for the Q&A session

At this point, you may wonder: aren't you studying the eSports spectator? As direct participants of eSports tournaments, aren't competitive gamers not spectators? This is where we notice the dynamic of the 'player/spectator hybrid' (Ditsmarch 2013, p. 22) which posits that spectators are often players of the game they spectate. This is especially keen in competitive gamers:

> "Back when I started competitively, I watched all of them (the various tournament leagues in LoL)." – ex-competitive gamer, interviewee no.2

As a competitive gamer, it is practically a necessity to spectate, in order to keep up with gameplay strategies and meta. The level of commitment required to be a competitive gamer is certainly not to be reckoned with, as interviewees comment on their experiences:

> "When you come in to play it's a lot more stressful, you're always worried about like how you know, how you're gonna' play, whether you're gonna' look awful." –competitive gamer, interviewee no. 10
> "It was stressful stuff, like playing 10 hours a day and stuff..." – ex-competitive gamer, interviewee no.6

Event Organisers

Many eSports events that take place are not official events organised by game companies. There exists fan-organised events, often in the form of localised viewing parties and tournaments. These events are the brainchild of Event Organisers. MOG MOBAR, one of the events I attended as part of my fieldwork, is a prime example of one such event- in fact, during LoL Worlds Finals 2014, there were three other similar viewing events held across Melbourne alone, each of which attracted a sizeable crowd of hundreds.

Such spectator participation and projects, as mentioned by Scholz (2012), are characteristic of a flourishing eSports scene. It is certainly no mean feat to organise such events – planning, garnering support and sponsorship, ticketing, and the actual legwork in ensuring the event runs smoothly on the day itself. On top of that, these fan event organisers usually have their own work, study or other commitments.

It is the substantial work done and time and commitment needed for such activities that brings up the debate on co-creative activities as free labour. Yet, it should be noted that some event organisers actually profit from events, although not-for-profit events exist as well.

> "For one, one of my life goals, it sounds a bit retarded, it's just, I want eSports in Australia to succeed... The reason I'm doing this viewing event specifically, is to get the community involved. To get the people to hang out together and socialise... I know that Riot supports us, so I know I can make their (the spectators) experience ten times better by having a group of, tons of other people being there." – not-for-profit viewing event organiser, Interviewee no.2

Event Volunteers

Photograph 5: Event volunteer arranging giveaway merchandise at MOG MOBAR 2014

Event volunteers are similar to organisers, in that they commit their time as helpers in running events for the masses. Their level of commitment is usually lower, with a more hands-on approach in preparing and running the event. During MOG MOBAR, there were various event volunteers taking on tasks such as hosting, door duty, facilitating the 2v2 gaming area, photographers and so on. These event volunteers play a key role in events; like cogs in a machine, their presence ensuring a smooth event experience.

> "Yeah, because I really like meeting new people, and I think meeting more people that play games is fun, can play with different people and stuff, and I like the community and I think that getting involved is pretty interesting, and I wouldn't mind spending more time meeting more people within, that play League of Legends, and help growing the community." – Event Volunteer, Interviewee No.7

Hosts/Emcees

Hosts/ emcees have the job of hyping up the crowd and managing the flow of the event, taking centre stage as they perform their role. Oftentimes, hosts are skilled not just in public speaking but in their knowledge of the game and the community. At PAX, the host was Riot Games' Oceanic Community Programs Coordinator, a full-time Riot staff. However for MOG MOBAR the hosts were event volunteers who took turns going onstage to carry out various activities such as hyping up the crowd for Worlds, hosting quizzes, conducting giveaways, being the loudspeaker for event proceedings. Both hosts have previous experience in hosting at official LoL tournaments - they also happen to be active content creators, carrying out activities such as vlogging, streaming or shoutcasting. I had the opportunity to speak briefly to one of the hosts, who mentioned her interest in pursuing a full-time career as an eSports event host- not just for LoL but other eSports titles.

Content Creators

Content creators consist of your streamers, video producers, and even those creating and distributing content on social media or websites – they are a fine example of how the eSports spectator experience is not limited to the literal event spectatorship, as spectators can continue to engage in broader spatial and temporal contexts. The existence of content creators falls within some of the characteristics of a flourishing eSports scene (Scholz 2012) - as content creators interact within communities, and provide 'journalistic coverage' of happenings within the scene. Content creators can play a crucial role in engaging and activating continued interest in the eSports community- audiences are often willing to consume, and at times, pay a premium in order to do so (as with Twitch paid subscriptions).

> "Yeah when I don't watch I read the news on the games that have been played, and I guess I follow the eSports scene of League of Legends in general. I use Reddit, because all the latest information is usually on that site, and sometimes the League of Legends site itself would have its own promotion of the eSports scene, and they would also have information about teams and what's going on in the scene." – Interviewee no. 7

Online Community Managers

Prevalent in the Oceanic eSports community is the presence of online communities. Noticeably many reside on Facebook groups or pages, created by moderated by fans. They provide a platform for the sharing of news, interaction between community members, and discussion between fans. Often, these sites can be localised, for example the group 'League of Legends Melbourne' or 'Summoner's Society (OCE)', building a local community space. Community space is extremely useful in facilitating an active community from which interest in the eSports scene and the game itself can be activated or sustained. For example, MOG MOBAR had advertised on localised Facebook groups, gaining support for their event. On top of that, such communities can even facilitate participants to become more involved, as per my interviewee's experience on having played competitively at a time:

> "So I got in a couple of Facebook groups, like Australian league players and that sort of thing, and there was a couple of people that were talking about you know, state teams and that sort of stuff, at that time I was a uni student so I didn't have a job, so I was like oh, that's okay, I guess I have time, so yeah I joined the Queensland team after tryouts and stuff, so I played there for a while" – Interviewee no.6

Cosplayers

Photograph 6: Cosplayers onstage at PAX AUS 2014

Cosplay, short for "costume play", is an activity where participants dress up in order to represent a certain character. Cosplayers are an integral part of live eSports events- generally parading around the event in-character, taking photos with event participants, at times giving performances onstage, and overall adding to the event atmosphere.

Cosplayers were out in full force at PAX- hundreds of cosplayers made their appearance. I myself was awed by the impressive cosplay, for it felt like the game champions had come to life. Even less true-to-character cosplays (e.g. males cross-dressing as female champions) were still visually engaging or entertaining. Many of these participated in a cosplay showcase held by Riot Games onstage, a segment that proved to be popular as audiences cheered, applauded and took photographs.

Photograph 7: Spectators watching the Oceanic Pro League tournament at League of Legends PAX AUS 2014

Last but not least are the eSports spectators. Their degree of participation is often overlooked, despite being the reason for which eSports exists.

To make clear how the role of 'spectator-in-play' is defined, I find it useful to bring in the ludological concept of the 'magic circle'- the imaginary space in which play occurs. The spectator is considered to be in the magic circle if they are committed to the in-game values, invested in the tension of play, and share a vicarious relationship with the player- and these spectators in the magic circle are those which I consider to take on the role of 'spectator-in-play'.

At PAX AUS, the amount of spectators that turned up was overwhelming- the benches were fully occupied, spectators stood along the perimeter. Spectators turned up in game memorabilia, or that of eSports teams that they support. When watching the eSports tournament, the air is thick with anticipation and excitement- as the tournament begins, even before any action in-game takes place, spectators cheer, collectively stirring up the atmosphere. Some spectators were observed explaining the background of the teams to others, or sharing which teams they support. Various reactionary performances take place upon the occurrence of in-game action- 'First Blood' (first kill of the game', achieving of in-game objectives (such as destroying towers) and good or bad plays (good plays meaning well-executed moves made in-game, the opposite for bad plays) all elicit loud responses, be it clapping, cheering, yelling or cries of oohs and ahhs. Even if one is not a skilled player of the game and does not entirely understand the play in-game, the enthusiasm of the crowd can be infectious.

Photograph 8: Spectators in LoL merchandise spectating League of Legends at PAX AUS 2014

There were many similar reactionary performances by the crowd that took place during MOG MOBAR's live stream of Worlds. When I casually asked some fellow viewers why they decided to attend the event, several mentioned the atmosphere ("Gotta' get pumped!"), whereas one mentioned that he wanted to meet people and make friends as well.

I cannot stress enough the impact of the presence of these spectators-in-play, and this is a notion shared by my interviewees:

"I prefer to watch it with people because its definitely more, you get more of the environment, if you just watch at home by yourself its just by yourself, and even if you see a very exciting moment, you can't share it with anyone, but if you're with people you can be like 'Oh my god it's a good play!' and things like that. It's the interactions with people as well."
– Interviewee no.3

Notably, the presence of spectators can impact the behaviour of the competitive gamer as well:

"Yeah when people are watching you wanna make it entertaining for them, but at the end of the day you still wanna win so you don't wanna go into any silly troll builds" – Interviewee no. 10

Values for participation

When looking at the values for participation, it would be more useful to bring in a specific scenario as example, on the basis that participatory roles within the ecosystem are dynamic and in flux- as spectators are often not consistent or fixed in the roles they uptake, and the meanings and values accorded to these roles can often change according to the scenario at hand.

As such, I decided to bring in the example of fan-organised LoL viewing event MOG MOBAR, showcasing the interrelation between the functions and roles that spectators may uptake, developing upon the spectator participatory ecosystem diagram:

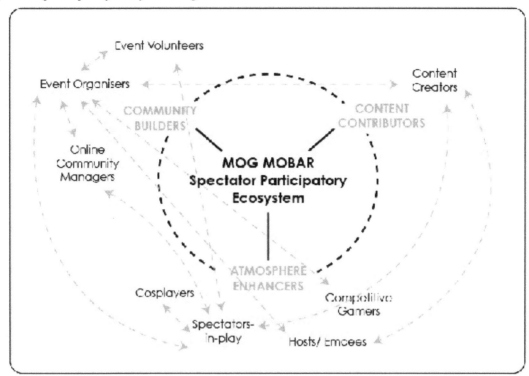

Diagram 2: Model of Spectator Participatory Ecosystem (MOG MOBAR) – with interrelation of roles

As you can see in the diagram, MOG MOBAR displays an active participatory ecosystem in which spectators take on various roles that contribute to the overall experience. The 'Content Contributors', 'Atmosphere Enhancers' and 'Community Builders' (outlined in green font) are the main functions of the various participatory roles that spectators take. These functions are joined in a dotted circle because they are interrelated- not only in how they work together to form the eSports experience, but also in how the functions can be fluid and overlap as spectators develop additional or new meanings in their own or other spectators' participatory roles. For example, whilst content creators are valuable for their content contribution (which can bring in many specific benefits such as educating the community, marketing an event, and so on), the content created may also aid in enhancing the atmosphere of an event. My observation of the MOG MOBAR event found that the content creation of videos about the MOBAR prior to the event- such as that produced by MOG itself, which gave an overview of what would happen at the event, various members that will be present, and other details- helped contribute in educating and marketing to the public the viewing party and various segments (and community members) of interest, activate continued interest and participation in the eSports community, and also in hyping up anticipation for the event itself, thus although coming in the main form and function of content contribution, it also aids in the functions of community building and atmosphere enhancing.

The grey arrows within the diagram refer to the various interrelations and interdependencies within the spectator ecosystem- revealing active spectators to be part of a highly social and self-representative network, from which they work together to generate meaning and their identities through their activities. This network once again brings in once again the notion of the interrelated ties between spectators in their roles, where many of these roles undertaken (and activities carried out) would not be able to sustain or remain meaningful without their fellow participants. For example, the MOG event organisers depend on many of the other active spectators to perform functions and thus give meaning to their role as organiser- they would require event volunteers to help with the footwork of the event, cosplayers, hosts/emcees and competitive gamers to hype up the event, spectators-in-play to support and attend the event, online community managers to provide the platforms from which they can advertise and interact with the community, content creators to create content on their event. Mutually, these actors also depend on the event organiser to provide a platform, a frame through which they are able to develop their identities- this interchange is most clearly seen in the cross-promotion of competitive gamers and the event.

Yet, these identities can be dynamic, with spectators traversing or harmonising various roles in their participation. I've outlined the fluidity of roles that spectators take in the following diagram:

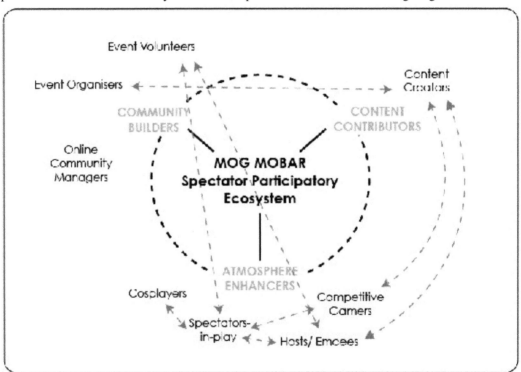

Diagram 3: Model of Spectator Participatory Ecosystem (MOG MOBAR) – with fluidity in roles

During MOG MOBAR, it was clear that spectators did not have rigid roles in their participation- the red arrows outline some of the observed duality or multiplicity of roles taken by some of the spectators. For example, the hosts and the competitive gamers attending the event also helped in content creation- not only by participating in MOG promotional videos and also in producing their own shout-out videos telling people of their involvement in the event and promoting the event. Notably, it also happens that the (voluntary) hosts of the event, outside of the event itself, not only identify as eSports event hosts, but also as eSports content creators, both having public Facebook pages listing roles such as 'shoutcaster' or 'vlogger'. During the event, they also took up the role of spectators-in-play, as once the tournaments began streaming, they too were focused on the in-game happenings on-screen. This shows us how active spectators are able to construct their own experiences and identities in a dynamic manner, allowing them to pursue and harmonise their different roles within the ecosystem.

Commodification of Spectator Participation

When considering the value of the participatory activities that spectators uptake, perhaps the most telling approach would be to consider how the eSports experience would be like without the ecosystem of spectator participation. Even if you left in the most basic elements such as eSports competitive gamers and spectators who watch, what is left would be a barren wasteland of an eSports experience, unlikely to sustain nor reach the height of popularity that LoL eSports is now experiencing.

The contribution of a healthy participatory ecosystem of spectators is immeasurable- it builds social networks, identities and communities around eSports, creates memorable experiences for consumers, activates and engages consumers on a broader temporal and spatial context beyond the game itself (but still linking with the game), all of which work together to create a sustainable and thriving experiential eSports scene leading to consumers' continuous identification and involvement with, loyalty and support of the game itself.

But let's not forget- the eSports scene was not built for the benefit of the spectators themselves. It was founded with a commercial purpose- as well put by one of my interviewees:

> "I guess you can say Riot is responsible for trying to make the scene succeed because that is what they want. An eSports scene makes people buy, makes people want to spend money on the game, or want to become better, makes you want to play more, that's the reason why there's an eSports scene. It's not made to profit pretty much, it's to made for them to create this dream for the casual player that they would become the best one day." – Interviewee no.2

The more successful the eSports scene, the higher the involvement with the game, the more money spent on the game and thus more profit for the game company. Indirectly, spectators are paying (through the game) for the eSports experience. This can be understood from the perspective of an experience economy- given that eSports is very much an experiential product, there is economic value for the game company to gain, from the co-creative participatory activities that spectators undertake in constructing and enhancing their own and the overall eSports experience.

Notably, there is demand for the rich eSports experience, as considerable amounts of consumers are willing to fork out money in order to attend eSports events- for example, both MOG MOBAR and PAX are ticketed events, going at AUD30-42 and AUD55-150 (early bird) respectively.

From the present situation of League of Legends eSports, it can be observed that Riot Games uses eSports primarily as a marketing vehicle- both in promoting the game and in sustaining interest, involvement and loyalty to the game rather than directing profiting from the eSports experience (e.g. by charging spectators to watch eSports content).

To some extent, Riot Games appears to recognise the value of co-creative participatory activity that spectators undertake, and makes efforts to encourage such activities.

"A cool thing that they were doing for all the cosplayers who participated in the cosplay parade, was that they gave like a gift pack basically. So it's like either a Tibbers pillow or Baron pillow, Teemo hat, and a few like soft toys, like little poros and stuff like that, the squishy toys, and some lanyards as well. They gave that, and it wasn't just to like a few. They gave to like hundreds of people." – Cosplayer, Interviewee no.11

Whereas another way would be by sponsorship and showing support for participatory activities:

"Actually the first time I cosplayed League was in Sydney... they thought it was really good, so they (Riot Games) sponsored my 3-day tickets into the event (PAX) in Melbourne. So yeah, it was like a savings of a hundred fifty dollars or so." – Cosplayer, Interviewee no.11
"I guess you could say we're kind of at the forefront of improving the play experience for Riot, but Riot gives us the tools to do that. In other words, if I didn't have that, all that swag (term standing for 'merchandise'), the play experience wouldn't be as good, pretty much. We being supported by Riot to make the experience better... they provide a lot of the tools to do a lot more, and that helps us give back." – Event Organiser, Interviewee no.2

The fact that Riot Games does not directly monetarily reward participatory activity might bring up the idea that these participatory spectators are being exploited for their labour- or conversely, it is possible that Riot Games recognises that motivations to participate are not necessarily commercial, and are attempting to navigate the dynamic, co-creative relationship between them and the participants in a manner that would satisfy both parties.

In any case, the eSports experience is indeed an experiential commodity belonging to the game company that active eSports spectators are making substantial contributions to, which Riot Games is currently capitalising on, resulting in a wildly popular and successful League of Legends.

Conclusion

The aim of this thesis was to investigate the role of the eSports spectator, following the line of questioning:

How do eSports spectators participate and make sense of their own eSports experience, how does this participation contribute to co-creating the overall 'eSports experience', and what is the resulting value for the eSports game company?

My case study into the Oceanic League of Legends eSports scene has answered the above questions-providing an ethnographic account of the various participatory roles undertaken by eSports spectators, and uncovering a strong participatory culture which can be seen through a highly social, networked eco-system through which spectators generate meaning and value in their participation with eSports, which I have laid out through the development of a model of the spectator participatory ecosystem. The spectator participatory ecosystem, when applied to specific scenarios, is useful in understanding the contributions, fluidity and interrelations between the roles and activities that eSports spectators undertake.

By looking at the various participatory roles identified in this research, and how they work together in an ecosystem consisting of many other active spectators, it is observable that not only does the individual spectator contribute to constructing their own eSports experience through the uptake of such roles, they also contribute to the formation of the overall eSports experience- making it clear that spectators do indeed play a key role in the eSports experience.

This key role and contribution of spectators creates economic value for the eSports game company, as a healthy spectator participatory ecosystem builds social networks, identities and communities around eSports, creates memorable experiences for consumers, activates and engages consumers on a broader temporal and spatial context beyond the game itself (but still linking with the game via affectivity and embodiment)- creating a thriving eSports scene which the game company capitalises upon, generating attention to the game, and gaining loyal consumers which continuously affiliate, engage and are highly involved with the game, and who thus support and spend on the game itself.

There are some implications to this- in allowing for spectators to play such a key role in co-creating the eSports experience, the game company is not wholly in control over the experience, and the resulting popularity of the eSports scene. For spectators, there is the issue of exploitation by the game company, as they contribute via their labour substantially to the final assemblage of the eSports scene, but for the most part, do not receive financial compensation for doing so. There may come a time when eventually spectators are fatigued from their roles, and back down from participation- potentially leading to a collapse of the healthy ecosystem. As such, it would be in the best interest of the game company to encourage and sustain the participatory culture and manage dynamic co-creative relationships in order to ensure a continual creation of economic value through the eSports experience.

Undeniably, there are various limitations to the research conducted for the purposes of this thesis. For one, eSports- and especially eSports spectatorship- is a relatively emergent field of research, therefore there is a limited body of academic research from which I am able to draw from. There is a heavy reliance on my own fieldwork to develop an understanding of the field- yet the nature of this project constrains the scale of research that I can undertake, limiting it to participation-observation over a short period of time (Oct'14-April'15), with focus on only two eSports events, and a small sample of 11 interviewees.

However, this study is suitable when taken as an exploratory research into the field, and contributes insight by laying down some initial groundwork and observations and an understanding of the key role that eSports spectators play, as well as in contributing to the larger discourses of participatory culture, co-creation and the experience economy. With that in mind, there is certainly room for further, larger-scale research on eSports spectatorship, examining, expanding upon or even extending beyond the initial findings of this study.

Brenda Ho graduated from the University of Melbourne with a B.A. in Media and Communications with First Class Honours, having completed her thesis under the supervision of Dr. Xin Gu. Upon graduation, she continues to live and breathe the online universe - only now less for defeating mobs and more for her bread and butter of being a Digital Strategist for a variety of awesome brands. Always game for a chat, she can be contacted at hokaiszebrenda@gmail.com

References

Atkinson, R. & Flint, J. (2004). Snowball Sampling. In Lewis-Beck, M.S., Bryman A., & Liao T.F. (Eds.), Encyclopaedia of Social Science Research Methods (pp. 1044-1045). California, USA: SAGE Publications, Inc.

Barberie, S. & Llamas, S. (2014) eSports: Digital Games Market Trends Brief. Super Data Digital games market intelligence. Retrieved May 16, 2014, from: http://www.superdataresearch.com/blog/esports-brief/

Banks, J.A. & Humphreys, S.M. (2008). The Labour of User Co-Creation, Emerging Social Network Markets?. The International Journal of Research into New Media Technologies 14(4), 401-418.

Benkler, Y. (2006). The Wealth of Networks: How Social Production Transforms Markets and Freedom. New Haven and London: Yale University Press.

Brennen, B.S. (2013). Qualitative Research Methods for Media Studies. New York, USA: Routledge, New York; London.

Borowy, M. & Jin, D.Y. (2013). Pioneering E-Sport: The Experience Economy and the Marketing of Early 1980s Arcade Gaming Contests. International Journal of Communication 7, 2254-2274.

Bruns, A. (2006). Towards Produsage: Futures for User-Led Content Production. In Proceedings Cultural Attitudes towards Communication and Technology 2006, 275-284.

Cheung, G. & Huang, J. (2011). Starcraft from the Stands: Understanding the Game Spectator. Proceedings of CHI Conference on Human Factors in Computing Systems, 763-772.

Crawford, G. (2004). Consuming sport: fans, sport and culture. London, UK: Routledge.

Ditsmarch, J.V. (2013). Video Games as a Spectator Sport: How Electronic Sports Transforms Spectatorship. Master's thesis, Utrecht University.

Dovey, J. & Kennedy H.W. (2006). Game Cultures: Computer Games as New Media. UK: Open University Press.

Hutchins, B. (2008). Signs of meta-change in second modernity: The growth of e-sport and the World Cyber Games. New Media and Society 10(6), 851-869.

Ind, N., Fuller, C., & Trevail, C. (2012). Brand Together: how co-creation generates innovation and re-energizes brands. London, UK: Kogan Page.

Jenkins, H. (2006). Convergence Culture: Where Old and New Media Collide. New York, USA: New York University Press.

Jenkins, H., Purushotma, R., & Weigel, M., Clinton, K., Robison A.J. (2009). Confronting the challenges of participatory culture: media challenges for the 21st century. Massachusetts, USA: The MIT Press.

Jenkins, H., Ford, S., Green, J. (2013). Spreadable media: creating value and meaning in a networked culture. New York, USA: New York University Press.

Jin, D.Y. (2010). Korea's Online Gaming Empire. London, UK: The MIT Press.

Jonnason, K. & Thiborg, J. (2010). Electronic sport and its impact on future sport. Sport in Society 13(2). 287-299.

Kow, Y.M. & Young, T. (2013). Media Technologies and Learning in the StarCraft eSport Community. Proceedings of CSCW 2013, 387-398.

Ludvigsen, M. & Veersawmy, R. (2010). Designing Technology for Active Spectator Experiences at Sporting Events. Proceedings of the 22nd Conference of the Computer-human Interaction Special Interest Group of Australia, 96-103.

Merriam, S.B. (2014). Qualitative Research: A Guide to Design and Implementation. San Francisco, USA: John Wiley & Sons, Inc.

Mora, P., & Héas, S. (2005). From videogamer to e-sportsman: Toward a growing professionalism of world-class players. In Metteo, B., Morris, S.C., & Nolan, M. (Eds.), Doom: Giocare in Prima Persona. Retrieved August 27, 2014, from http://emmijaphi.pagesperso-orange.fr/esport/fichiers/moraheas.pdf

Pine, B.J. II & Gilmore, J.H. (1998). Welcome to the Experience Economy. Harvard Business Review 76(4). 97-105.

Pine, B.J. II & Gilmore, J.H. (2013). The experience economy: past, present and future. In Sundbo, J., & Sørensen, F. (Eds.), Handbook on the Experience Economy (pp.1-17). Gloucestershire, UK: Edward Elgar Publishing Limited.

Rambusch, J., Jakobsson, P., & Pargman, D. (2007). Exploring E-sports: A Case Study of Gameplay in Counter-Strike. Proceedings of DiGRA 2007 Conference, 157-164.

Reeves, S., Brown, B., & Laurier, E. (2009). Experts at play: Understanding skilled expertise. Games and Culture 4(3), 205-227.

Riot, M. (2014). What are the 2014 Regional Qualifiers?. Retrieved April 1, 2015, from: http://na.leagueoflegends.com/en/news/esports/esports-event/what-are-2014-regional-qualifiers.

Roig, A., San Cornelio, G., Sánchez-Navvaro, J., & Ardèvol, E. (2014). The fruits of my own labor: A case study on clashing models of co-creativity in the new media landscape. International Journal of Cultural Studies

17(6). 637-653.

Salen, K. & Zimmerman, E. (2004). Rules of play: game design fundamentals. Massachusetts, USA: The MIT Press.

Scholz, T.M. (2011). New Broadcasting Ways in IPTV- The Case of the StarCraft Broadcasting Scene. In Christophers, J. & Scholz, T.M. (Eds.), eSports Yearbook 2011/2012 (pp.89-105). Norderstedt, Deutschland: Books on Demand GmbH.

Schwartz, N. (2014). More people watch eSports than watch the World Series or NBA Finals. USA TODAY 19 May 2014. Retrieved September 22, 2014, from: http://ftw. usatoday.com/2014/05/league-of-legends-popularity-world-series-nba.

Seo, Y. (2013). Electronic sports: A new marketing landscape of the experience economy. Journal of Marketing Management 29, 1542-1560.

Sundbo, J., & Sørensen, F. (2013). Introduction to the experience economy. In Sundbo, J., & Sørensen, F. (Eds.), Handbook on the Experience Economy (pp.1-17). Gloucestershire, UK: Edward Elgar Publishing Limited.

Tassi, P. (2013). The U.S. Now Recognizes eSports Players as Professional Athletes. Forbes 15 July 2013. Retrieved May 16, 2014, from: http://www.forbes.com/sites/insertcoin/2013/07/14/the-u-s-now-recognizes-esports-players-as-professional-athletes/.

Taylor, T.L., & Witkowski, E. (2010). This is How We Play It: What a Mega-LAN Can Teach Us About Games. International Conference on Foundations of Digital Games 2010, 195- 202.

Taylor, T.L. (2012). Raising the Stakes: The Professionalization of Computer Gaming. London, UK: The MIT Press, London.

Vang, J., & Tschang, T. (2013). Unpacking the spatial organization of the US videogames industry: lessons for research on experience industry clusters. In Sundbo, J., & Sørensen, F. (Eds.), Handbook on the Experience Economy (pp.1-17). Gloucestershire, UK: Edward Elgar Publishing Limited.

Wagner, M. (2006). On the Scientific Relevance of eSports. Proceedings of the 2006 International Conference on Internet Computing and Conference on Computer Game Development.

Witkowski, E. (2009). Probing the sportiness of eSports. In Christophers, J., & Scholz, T. (Eds.), eSports yearbook 2009 (pp.53-56). Norderstedt, Deutschland: Books on Demand GmbH.

Witkowski, E. (2012). Inside the Huddle: The Sociology and Phenomenology of Team Play in Networked Computer Games. PhD thesis, IT University of Copenhagen.

Informal Roles within eSport Teams: A Content Analysis of the Game Counter-Strike: Global Offensive

By Rolf Drenthe

Considerable research has focussed on formal roles in traditional sports, with the aim to better understand the development of roles, the benefits of having clear roles and the detrimental or negative effects that underdeveloped roles in teams can have. However, the study of informal roles has received less attention: In 2011 Cope, Eys, Beauchamp, Schinke & Bosselut, have looked into informal roles within traditional sports. Before going into the present study and informal roles it is important to understand formal roles and role development.

Formal roles are referred to the expectations about patterns of behaviours for an individual in a social structure (McGrath 1984; Shaw & Costanzo 1982; Sherif & Sherif 1953) and can be defined as features of teams and groups (Salas, Dickinson, Converse & Tannenbaum 1992; Sherif & Sherif 1969). The roles can arise from the position, status and/or assumed responsibilities within a current situation (Carron, Hausenblas, & Eys, 2005). In 1966, Bales explains role development through behaviours of the role necessity. Three types of behaviour were observed that could be associated with different roles within a task-orientated team. (1) 'Activity' which is the degree to which an individual performs behaviours directed towards standing out from others, (2) 'Task ability' which is the degree to which an individual demonstrates expertise toward group goal attainment, and (3) 'likeability' which can be seen as the degree to which an individual performs behaviours directed towards the development and maintenance of socially satisfying relationships. The degree a individual inherits these three behaviours influences the potential roles that person will occupy in a group. As an example Bales states that a person who has all three types will more likely fulfill a leadership role while in contrast someone who exhibits none of these behaviours would be an 'underactive deviant' role.

Another theory looks into the communication framework regarding roles. It consist of a person with authority (i.e., role sender) to a subordinate (i.e., focal person). This framework as seen in figure 1 was originally developed Kahn et al. (1964) and further by Eys, Carron, Beauchamp & Bray (2005). This role responsibility communication process consist of five consecutive events. The first event is that the role sender (e.g., the coach or a teammate) creates an expectation of a role for the focal person (e.g., athlete). The event after this is where the sender communicates these expectations to the focal person (i.e., places role pressure on focal person). The third event, occurs when the focal person perceives this role pressure and at that moment the focal person assesses if the communication or expectations are clear.

First the role sender (e.g., the coach or teammate) develops expectations for the focal person (i.e., the athlete). After that, the role sender communicates these expectations to the focal person. The third event occurs at the point the focal person experiences or perceives the expectations that have been placed upon him or her. At this moment the focal person assesses if the communication or expectations are clear or unclear. Event four is the response of the focal person regarding the expectations, this response can include many forms including behaviours, such as compliance or rejection, cognitions, such as raised or lowered efficacy beliefs (Eys & Carron 2001), and anxiety or dissatisfaction (Beauchamp et al. 2003b; Eys, Carron, Beauchamp & Bray 2003). The last event is where the role sender interprets the response, and where the role sender have to reflect and evaluate and either maintain or change their role expectations and starting the sequence again from event one.

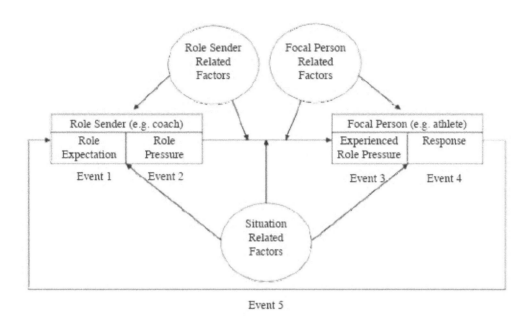

Figure 1: A Theoretical Framework of Factors Influencing the Transmission and Reception of Role Responsibilities (Eys, Carron, Beauchamp & Bray 2005)

Next to the five events within the same framework, there are three categories that can influence the focal person's understanding regarding their role. The lack of clear understanding of their role is called role ambiguity (Kahn, Wolfe, Quinn, Snoek & Rosenthal 1964). Role ambiguity is associated with the decrease in the perception of task cohesion and self-efficacy (Eys & Carron 2001). And it also reflects the role satisfaction (Beauchamp, Bray, Eys & Carron 2003a), the athlete's overall satisfaction (Eys, Carron, Bray & Beauchamp 2003), and the role performance (Beauchamp, Bray, Eys & Carron 2002; Bray & Brawley 2002). Also the perception of intensity regarding state anxiety has been connected to role ambiguity (Beauchamp et al., 2003b). The first category, is role sender related factors, deals with the sources of the athlete's role ambiguity that might be attributed to, or are in direct control of, the role sender (e.g., a coach). For example the quantity and quality of the verbal communication by the coach towards the athlete might be poor, which can lead to ambiguity. The second category is about focal person related factors, which can serve as the source of role ambiguity that might be attributed to, or are in control of the focal person (e.g., the athlete). For example, an athlete who is new in a certain sport might be confused by the terminology used, because of the lack of experience within that sport. The last category situation related factors, serve as a source of role ambiguity that are not controlled by the focal person or the role sender. An example could be the time the athlete has been on the team. Role ambiguity has shown to be higher at the beginning of a competitive season than at the end (Eys, Carron, Beauchamp & Bray 2003).

There is also role conflict which is a conflict related to that a person is having too many roles, next to that it can be caused by other people that expect different things (i.e., roles) from the same person (Weinberg and Gould, 2011). The following quote by a 36 year old non-traditional college athlete who was also a mother of two children, will illustrate this type of conflict.

> "The whole week my son was sick, I hardly trained at all. I would have to wait until my husband came home from work, but sometimes he would work a double shift so I would get no running in. So not only was my training hurt but I missed several classes because I had to stay home with my son" (Jambor & Weeks 1996, p.150)

The above explained negatives consistently show that they are linked to a higher job-related tension, reduction in organizational commitment, job dissatisfaction, and impaired performance (Fisher & Gitelson 1983; Jackson & Schuler 1986; Van Sell, Brief, & Schuler 1981) and burnouts (e.g., Barling & MacIntyre 1993). Even though these researches have been mostly carried out with work roles (e.g., Supervisors, managers) within organizations (cf. King & King 1990), it was found that role ambiguity also had negative associations with role-related efficacy beliefs within interdependent sport teams (Beauchamp & Bray 2001).

Lauri Mains (Coach of the New Zealand All Black international rugby team) commented on his efforts to reduce role ambiguity: "Everyone knows what he has to do in each given situation, this is brought about. By building on a basic philosophy so that he can make decisions at the time when he needs to" (Quotes in Mconnel 1999, p. 146). In regards with reducing role conflict, it seems that successful teams ensured that individuals recognize that their contribution has an importance as well as the value, as well as the value of each other team member. Mark Messier (Mabry & Barnes 1980), a former team member of Wayne Gretzky, said "I never felt I was playing in [Gretzky's] shadow. I had a responsibility on the team that was different from Wayne's. Everyone had his role, and I felt great about mine. So did many other about theirs. If we won, and won often, we knew everyone would get respect." (p. 60).

However, the above research is mostly based on formal roles, but roles can also be informal (Mabry & Barnes 1980). As stated earlier, formal roles are those that are established by an organization or a group and are typically connected to an objective of the group. Informal roles on the other hand are being developed through the interaction between group members and are not formally assigned by the group or organization (Mabry & Barnes 1980). Cope et al. (2011) have looked into the informal roles within traditional sports (e.g. football, & basketball), and they have identified and defined 12 informal roles (See table 1). In Figure 2 the informal roles they found are placed in a continuum that ranges from most detrimental role (i.e., the cancer, M= -3.0 ± 1.3) to the most beneficial informal role (i.e., the mentor, M= 3.5 ± 0.8).

Informal role	Definition
Comedian	An athlete who entertains others through the use of comical situations, humorous dialogue, and practical jokes. This individual can also be referred to as a jokester, clown, or prankster.
Spark plug	An athlete who ignites, inspires, or animates a group toward a common goal. May be referred to as the task booster
Cancer	An athlete who expresses negative emotions that spread destructively throughout a team.
Distracter	An athlete who draws away or diverts the attention of other teammates decreasing their focus.
Enforcer	An athlete who is physically intimidating or willingly belligerent and who is counted on to retaliate when rough tactics are used by the opposing team.
Mentor	An athlete who acts as a trusted counselor or teacher for another athlete on the team. This athlete has usually been with the team for a few years and has experience and wisdom to teach the less experienced athlete(s).
Informal leader – nonverbal	An athlete who leads the team by example, hard work, and dedication.
Informal leader – verbal	An athlete who leads the team both on and off the playing surface through commands. This individual is not selected by the team as a leader but assumes the role through social interactions.
Team player	An athlete who gives exceptional effort and can be seen as a workhorse that is willing to sacrifice and put the team before his/her own well-being.
Star player	An athlete who is distinguished or celebrated because of their personality, performance, and/or showmanship.
Malingerer	An athlete who prolongs psychological or physical symptoms of injury for some type of external gain (e.g., sympathy, attention, access to athletic therapy).
Social convener	An athlete who is involved in the planning and organization of social gatherings for a team to increase group harmony and integration.

Table 1: Informal roles and definitions (Cope et al. 2011)

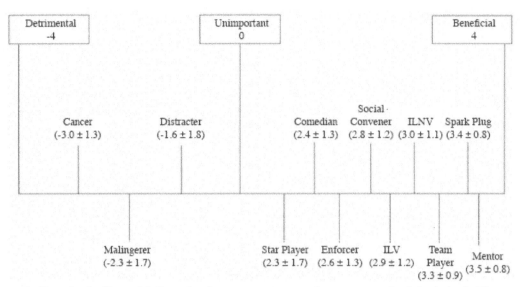

Figure 2: Perceived effect of informal roles on sport teams (mean ± standard deviation) (Cope et al. 2011).

Knowing that certain roles have a beneficial and detrimental contribution teams are able to focus on developing the positive roles more and limiting the negative roles to possibly increase the team's performance.

Aims

The aim of this study was to develop a better understanding regarding informal roles within the eSport setting. The study has explored if (1) it is possible to use audio analysis to identify informal roles and which roles within two professional Counter-Strike: Global Offensive eSport teams and (2) which communication factors might influence the development of clear informal role development.

The present study has analysed two Counter-Strike: Global Offensive (CS:GO) teams, by using open source audio data from the 2015 ESL Pro League. Data analysis started by transcribing the audio files, as the research had a analytic aim specific features of speech were left out (e.g., intonation, emotions). The researcher decided to stop coding when saturation of data was reached, this can have negative consequences as data could be missed.

Methodology

The present study used open source data from two top 10 Counter-Strike: Global Offensive (CS:GO) teams. The teams that were analysed were both native English with one participant in each team that had a mixed nationality. Ten total participants (five in each team), with an average age of 23,71 years (SD: 3,04). Three hours and 50 minutes were analysed, relevant time for the research was not calculated. The recordings all dated from the ESL Pro League 2015. The data of the present study only included the speech of the participating players.

The data was analysed by transcribing the speech of the players, specific features of speech such as volume, intonation and hearable emotions were left out due to the analytic aim of the research. Jenks (2011) and Kuckartz (2014) stated that in most social research a basic transcription system is sufficient and including features of interaction is not needed. However, after transcribing it was found that having these features might have added an extra dimension to the present study. In order to answer the researcher's questions a process of analysing qualitative information in a systematic manner by encoding qualitative data was used (i.e., Thematic analysis) (Boyatzis, 1998).

The themes for the researches came from Cope et al. (2011) (n=12). Next to this additional themes were developed during the research (N=12). In the end of the research five codes were removed, and three codes were grouped together, giving a total of 17 codes to be used.

Trustworthiness

The researcher decided that coding should stop when saturation appeared, and although he realized that by doing so there is a possibility that important data could be missed.

Trustworthiness has been enhanced by taking three of Maxwell's (2002) criteria for qualitative inquiries into consideration. These are descriptive validity, interpretive validity and generalizability. Descriptive validity was achieved by transcribing the audio recordings, interpretive validity by author, checks from the supervisors and peers with understanding of eSports. Generalizability was not achieved, as data was only collected from two teams competing in the same game.

Biases

The research admits that there is a possibility of slight bias regarding communication in eSport through own negative experience with communication in lower ranks of different games. However the researcher expects that communication and by that also role communication would have an increased quality in top ranking teams.

Results

The analysis of the transcripts showed that multiple roles were able to be found by using the audio recordings, certain roles were more dominantly present for example the team player and the informal leader verbal (ILV) compared to others such as the cancer or comedian. Also communicative features such as incomprehensible speech or multiple people speaking at the same time were more often found compared to roles. The results have been divided into two sections to make it easier to read. Section 4.1 would focus on the roles while section 4.2 would discuss the communicative features that were found. In the discussion the relationship between roles and communication will be explored.

In the upcoming part the results regarding to the twelve roles as described by Cope et al. (2011) will be shown separately.

Informal leader verbal

The informal leader verbal (ILV) can be described as "an athlete who leads the team both on and off the playing surface through commands. This individual is not selected by the team as a leader but assumes the role through social interaction." (Cope et al. 2011). Expressions that were related to the ILV were found during tactical preparation and giving orders. The following were a couple of quotes related to the tactical speech from the recordings: "Do Default, Default to mid control", "cap, four of us run up cap like we running up, jump off mid B just fucking it" and "Okay we gonna do it like we did against [a different team]". The first one could be interpret as a tactic to first start of with a default setting, switching to mid control. The second describes a tactic through different waypoints. And the last one is a reference to a previously used tactic. The last quote also caused some confusion to a different team member who needed to ask for clarification. It was also seen that the ILV in certain cases tried to be more democratic and asked the team what to do, for example "guys you want to start T or CT", another situation the ILV asked confirmation "I want you to smoke mid B late, we gonna do three at long and two cat okay?". Examples related to orders could be "Everyone else stay B with him [name]", "together, wait wait wait for your team" and "just keep holding". These commands reflect a style of giving orders to try and keep a certain tactic to work or response to communicative feedback from teammates.

Informal leader nonverbal

The informal leader nonverbal (ILNV) is defined as "An athlete who leads the team by example, hard work, and dedication." (Cope et al. 2011). In the present research this role was not found as the present study only used recordings from a spectator point of view rather than each individual player's point of view. It was thus not possible to filter the usage of quick commands.

Cancer

The cancer as defined by Cope et al. (2011) as "an athlete who expresses negative emotions that spread destructively throughout a team". This definition does not directly relate to negative or possible destructive comments & emotions. However, during analysis it showed that there were people acting like wiseacre's (people who think they know everything better). This was shown by a person saying "That is <not understandable> shitty smoke you thrown actually" and similar remarks. These kind of remarks could have a negative or even destructive impact on the person who executed this action. Another example of possible behaviour related to this role was "I knew that was gonna happen, I was trying to get us out of there". This can be interpret as a negative as he tries to make the team believe that the situation was going to happen after it actually happened. Another example situation that occurred was there was a discussion going on between two team members, one of the team members ended the discussion with the following comment "Whatever dude". This comment was verbally expressed as I don't care what you think, I know I am right but let's just move on. Even though this comment might have worked to stop the discussion and refocus on the game, it might also have a negative consequence on the team as a certain negative atmosphere has been developed.

Comedian

The comedian role as described by Cope et al. (2011) is "An athlete who entertains others through the use of comical situations, humorous dialogue, and practical jokes. This individual can also be referred to as a jokester, clown, or prankster.". This role was only found in a few situations. One of the situations was when the leader stated their tactic rather simple during the warming up round "Let's get mid control first and all that bullshit" a team member responded by stating "good post plans man". Both of these sentences could possibly be seen as a joke, even though the first sentence should have focussed on tactical speech, but due to stating "and all that bullshit" it could be interpreted as a joke. A joke was made out of it by stating "all that bullshit", while expecting at the same time that the team knows what to do. A different sentence was "They gonna do some crazy shit man" a teammate responded with "Yeah like they gonna die, but it gonna look really crazy". This also could be related to being a joke, by changing the wording of the team member and showing own confidence.

Team player

A team player is described as "An athlete who gives exceptional effort and can be seen as a workhorse that is willing to sacrifice and put the team before his/her own well-being" Cope et al. (2011). If going specifically at this definition only a few quotes were found that could be related to this role, such as" I am holding long [name]", "Go I will hold your flank" and "I can get long, I am leaving bomb for you guys". These quotes all got some sort of self-sacrifice in common. This is because covering a team member puts you in a more dangerous position but also going somewhere without the team may also put yourself in harm's way.

If looked at only giving exceptional effort, it might be said that calling out enemies and reporting one's own action can be considered to fall into this category. If this is the case then nearly all members of the observed teams would have the role of team player with a quote count of 420, divided over two codes(Calling out enemies, reporting own action & thought sharing). But it might also be perceived as a standard operation and thus not being specifically connected to being a team player. Examples of thought sharing are "he is just lurking just wait", and "could be pushing upper again". This clearly shows that team members share their thoughts about what the opposing team is doing. Next to that they call out the opposing team "last guy door, last guy door", "one is crossing now, two crossing" and "he is close left door I think". This can be beneficial for the other team members to know what is going on at certain places and times during the match, and can cause the team to adjust their tactic accordingly. The last possible related theme to a team player is stating one's own actions such as "I am going to go car", "Flashing mid right now" and "I am smoking A mid". Calling out what you are doing can most likely provide significant benefits, throwing a flash grenade (Flashing), without calling it out, can cause you to blind your own team mates.

Enforcer

The definition of the enforcer is "someone who is physically intimidating or willingly belligerent and who is counted on to retaliate when rough tactics are used by the opposing team". The present study shows that enforcers might also use verbal communication to enforce actions within their own team. As no direct physical aspect in present within eSports, verbal enforcing towards own team has been looked into as part of the enforcing role. Quotes like "Hey we can't have drinks on the table, I am pretty sure.", "focus on this round, focus on this round" and "Just hold mid, [name] hold upper B" all somehow trying to enforce something. The first quote tries to enforce the rules regarding the competition, the second one tries to stimulate but also enforce focus on the game. The last quote focusses on the tactic that had been discussed and telling the team members to adhere to that tactic.

Spark plug

The spark plug is a person who inspires team members towards a common goal, as such this person might use motivational cues to get them ready to perform their task. The following quotes could be interpreted as motivational "we are playing them perfect boys", "this is our f***ing map boys, this is what happens when they don't anti shred", "yeah let's do it", "here we go boys let's do this", "win this one and we are in the semi's" and "go , go a, only two a, you guys f***ing got this.".

Distracter

The distracter role described as "An athlete who draws away or diverts the attention of other teammates decreasing their focus" (Cope et al. 2011) was not directly found, situations where teammates were shouting, interrupting and talking at the same time as someone else, might be defined as a distraction.

Mentor

The mentor role as described by Cope et al. (2011) "An athlete who acts as a trusted counsellor or teacher for another athlete on the team. This athlete has usually been with the team for a few years and has experience and wisdom to teach the less experienced athlete(s)" was not found during this study. The cause of this could be that the role might not be the most effective during a high pressure situation. It is possible that this role does exist during training matches, though.

Star player

During the recordings no player was found to inhibit the star player role, described as an athlete who is distinguished or celebrated because of their personality, performance, and/or showmanship (Cope et al. 2011).

Malingerer

The malingerer described as "An athlete who is prolongs psychological or physical symptoms of injury for some type of external gain (E.g., sympathy, attention, access to athletic therapy)" (Cope et al. 2011) was not able to be identified. One athlete stated that his knee still hurts. However, it is uncertain if the athlete who prolongs his injury or if the injury occurred recently.

Social convener

The social convener was as expected not found during analysis. The role involves planning and organizing of social gatherings for the team to increase group harmony and integration (Cope et al., 2011). It is possible that this role is present after matches or during training or everyday life.

Communication

Even though looking into the communication was not the original aim of the research, it became an aim after finding so many communicational features. During the research the following characteristics were found: 1. Incomprehensible speech; 2. Fast speech; 3. Repeating speech; 4. Shouting; 5. Inefficient communication; 6. Multiple people talking.

Incomprehensible speech is anything that the researcher was unable to transcribe from the audio recordings caused by the speed of speech and/or the pronunciation, and thus can vary from one word to full sentences. The Incomprehensible speech unit was found 349 times within 2 transcripts.

The speech rate within eSports varies. It was calculated that the average was around 200 words per minute (WPM), and the highest rate was calculated at 365 WPM. Dugdale (N.d.) states that 130 to 200 words per minute is recommended for normal speech. The wpm was calculated as following, 60 seconds$\div x1=x3$, $x3 \times x2=WPM$. x1 is a speech section in seconds, x2 are the amount of words within this speech section. Below an example is given:

A section of 9 seconds was selected, within these 9 seconds there were a total of 38 words present. (60 seconds$\div 9=6,667$, $6,667 \times 38$ words$=253$ WPM.)

Repeating, interrupting and talking at the same time were found often during data analysis. It is recognized that repeating a word once can be pretty common, especially in a shooter game where it is important that the team knows what is going on. Repeating action and observation call out once will give the members an extra notice about what is going on. However, it was noticed that repeating statements occurred more than once, certain statements were repeated four to five times. These repetitions were marked as repetitive speech.

Another common problem was that members often talked at the same time. This was observed a total of 150 times. In certain cases a person was talking and got interrupted and in other cases two people started talking at the same time and continued to talk. In other cases it seems that players were not able to keep full attention to the communication as seen in the following dialogue:

> P1: drop him an opt, drop him an opt
> P1: scott AK charlie
> P2: you want me to drop him an opt
> P1: yeah drop him an opt

Within this dialogue P1 gives an order to another member to drop a weapon. The team member responds with the question "you want me to drop him an opt" This response can be interpreted in different ways, 1) the team member did not notice that someone was talking to him or 2) was not listening to the communication at all.

Conclusion and Discussion

The present study's purpose was to explore which informal roles are present in the professional eSport setting and specifically in the game Counter-Strike: Global Offensive. Audio recordings from two teams were analysed and even though each team's recording was a unique case, similarities between the two were found. The findings of the study suggest that voice communication analysis does allow for finding informal roles.

The findings of this study show that roles as the informal leader verbal, spark plug, distracter and the cancer are also found within the eSport setting. The informal leader verbal role is dominantly present, especially when listening for tactical speech or direct orders. Due to limitations in the research it could not be known if the holder of the informal leaders verbal role was in fact also the one who holds the formal role as team leader/captain. The spark plug was also found, but it was not possible to determine if the quotes found were also perceived motivational by the teams. The distractor was also present depending on the interpretation of draws away or diverts the attention. If a player is interrupting, talking at the same time or shouting, it could be interpreted as a distractor for certain people, but it might be possible that people who are used to this style of communication might not perceive it in a similar way. The cancer role was present in a form of a wiseacre (a know it all), the data does not conclude that this role is dominantly present within either of the two teams. Limited data showed the presence of the comedian role, even though it was expected that this role would be easily found. It is possible that the jokes within eSport are perceived significantly different for the researcher than for the participants. The role of team player was found, but only with a limited amount of quotes that would fulfill the 'sacrifice' and 'putting the team before his/her own well-being' of the definition. However, if a team player would be defined as a person who does everything in their power to support the team, it could be said that nearly all player, within the analysed teams would fulfill this role, as they call out the location of the opposing team and their own actions.

Certain roles do not match the definition that Cope et al. (2011) suggested, for the specific roles 'enforcer' and 'informal leader nonverbal' might need adapting to fit the eSport sector. The current definition of the enforcer role states that "it is an athlete who is physically intimidating or willingly belligerent and who is counted on to retaliate when rough tactics are used by the opposing team." However, in eSports there is no physical intimidation possible, this makes it so that this role does not appear in this specific way. It can be suggested that the enforcer role can have a second definition as "A player who is verbally intimidating and who is counted on to enforce the rules or tactics to make sure the group stays on task and does as expected." This description of the role comes close to that of the spark plug, which is the role that "ignites, inspires or animates a group towards a common goal." The difference is that the enforcer will enforce the rules to reach the goal, where the spark plug inspires thegroup. This can mean that there are two types of enforce rules exist. The 'informal leader nonverbal' role might needs adaptation, the present definition by Cope et al. (2011) state that the informal leader nonverbal is "an athlete who leads the team by example, hard work, and dedication", as non-verbal communication is possible within eSports in the form of pings or quick commands. Within Counter-Strike the form of quick commands is used, and are used in order to call out the opposing team, without using the voice of the actual player. Within multiplayer online battle arena (MOBA) games these commands are often referred to as pings, pings will result in showing your team members certain situations on the map such as if there is an enemy missing, if there is a need for assistance, if you are on your way, if there is danger or if there is a need to retreat. How often quick commands are used in Counter Strike has not been researched and as MOBA games were not included in the study, there is no data regarding the usage of pings. However it might be that a player who actively uses the ping system to inform or guide team members can be identified as a non-verbal leader and the suggestion to adapt the informal leader nonverbal role to "An athlete who leads the team by example, hard work, and dedication or by the usage of a significant amount of non-verbal communication". Feedback from players might provide beneficial in order to locate and distinguish roles, it is also possible that the limited amount of analysed audio recordings caused for the lack of found roles.

The data consisted mostly of communication units, and negative characteristics are prone to be found during high intensity moments, for optimal team performance it might be better to train communication in order to avoid these characteristics. Interruptions (i.e., People start talking while others are already talking, causing the first person to stop talking), multiple people talking (i.e., Two or more people talking at the same time), incomprehensive speech and fast speech were found by the researchers to distort most information and could cause distractions or the inability to comprehend possible necessary information that could lead the team to victory.

The theory regarding roles show that having clear role communication could provide benefits in performance, however over communicating and unclear communicating as found might be considered negative for the development of clear roles. Certain issues were encountered that reduced the quality of the present study and it is recommended for future research to account for these issues. Data collection within the eSport setting was rather difficult, during this study teams were perceived closed off, non-responded or if they state they are were willing to participate they withdrew without a notice. Due to the lack of active participants in the current study, the usage of open source recordings were used from the 2015 ESL ESEA Pro League. The usage of open source audio recording per se is not a problem. However, there is no control for certain influences such as; (1) it was not possible to isolate each player, (2) remove background noise which caused for a longer and harder time to transcribe the data and for data to get lost, due to noise. Having the ability to have each player and the in game sound on separate audio channels would significantly increase the quality of the data and with that the ability to analyse it. Next to having each sound input on a separate channel it might be useful to have each screen recorded, this will create the possibility to analyse non-verbal screen behaviour for each individual.

Next to the usage of open source audio recordings, the lack of participants for the current study caused that the quantitative part of the study could not be performed, which would have identified the informal roles from the perspective of the participants and would provide data regarding beneficial and detrimental levels for each role which would make comparison to the Cope et al. (2011) study possible. The lack of participants also has an impact on how generalizable the study is within the eSport sector. It might be important that future research to increase sample size, but also to collect data from practice, use the informal roles questionnaire and/or interviews from players to further clarify the informal roles in eSports. Next to this it might be interesting to look into how communication quality and quantity influences the role development.

In summary, the results suggest that similar informal roles are able to be found in eSport through the usage of voice communication with the exception of a few. Certain roles might need an adaptation in definition. Communication characteristics might influence the development of informal roles and with that decrease the performance of the teams. Next to that communication has influence on the quality of the research. Thus, communication training within eSports might benefit both the teams as well as the researchers.

Rolf Drenthe has graduated from the University of Jyväskylä in 2016 from the master program sport and exercise psychology. He followed his interest to do research in the field of eSport as this sport is becoming increasingly popular, but also because his own experience with the video gaming community.

References

Barling, J., & MacIntyre, A. T. (1993). Daily work role stressors, mood and emotional exhaustion. Work and Stress, 7(4), 315-325.

Beauchamp, M. R., Bray, S. R., Eys, M. A., & Carron, A. V. (2002). Role ambiguity, role efficacy, and role performance: Multidimensional and mediational relationships within interdependent sport teams. Group Dynamics: Theory, Research, and Practice, 6, 229-242.

Beauchamp, M. R., Bray, S. R., Eys, M. A., & Carron, A. V. (2003a). Multidimensional role ambiguity and role satisfaction: A prospective examination using interdependent sport teams. Manuscript submitted for publication, University of Leeds, Leeds, UK.

Beauchamp, M. R., Bray, S. R., Eys, M. A., & Carron, A. V. (2003b). The effect of role ambiguity on competitive state anxiety. Journal of Sport & Exercise Psychology, 25(1), 77-92.

Beauchamp, M. R., & Bray, S.R., (2001). Role ambiguity and role conflict within interdependent teams. Small Group Research, 32(2), 133-157.

Boyatzis, R.E. (1998). Transforming Qualitative Information: Thematic Analysis and Code Development. London, UK: Sage Publications.

Bray, S. R., & Brawley, L. R. (2002). Role clarity, role efficacy, and role performance effectiveness. Small Group Research, 33, 245-265.

Carron, A.V., Hausenblas, H.A., & Eys, M.A. (2005). Group dynamics in sport (3rd ed.). Morgantown, WV: Fitness Information Technology.

Cope, C. J., Eys, M. A., Beauchamp, M. R., Schinke, R. J., & Bosselut, G. (2011). Informal roles on sport teams. International Journal of Sport and Exercise Psychology, 9, 19–30.

Dugdale. (n.d.). What 's your speech rate. Retrieved March 21, 2016, from http://www.write-out-loud.com/speech-rate.html.

Eys, M. A., Carron, A. V, Beauchamp, M. R., & Bray, S. R. (2003). Role Ambiguity in Sport Teams. Journal of Sport & Exercise Psychology, 25, 534–550.

Eys, M. A., Carron, A. V., Bray, S. R., & Beauchamp, M. R. (2003). Role ambiguity and athlete satisfaction. Journal of Sports Sciences, 21(5), 391-401.

Eys, M.A., & Carron, A.V. (2001). Role ambiguity, task cohesion, and task self-efficacy. Small group research, 32, 356-373.

Eys, M.A., Carron, A.V., Beauchamp, M.R., & Bray, S.R. (2005) Athletes' perceptions of the sources of role ambiguity. Small Group Research, 36, 383-403.

Fisher, C. D., & Gitelson, R. (1983). A meta-analysis of the correlates of role conflict and ambiguity. Journal of Applied Psychology, 68(20), 320-333.

Jackson, S. E., & Schulder, R. S. (1985). A meta-analysis and conceptual critique of research on role ambiguity and role conflict in work settings. Organizational behaviour and human decision processes, 36, 16-78.

Jambor, E.A., & Weeks, E.M. (1996). The nontraditional female athlete: A case study. Journal of Applied Sport Psychology, 8, 146–159.

Jenks, C.J. (2011). Transcribing Talk and Interaction: Issues in the Representation of Communication Data. Amsterdam: John Benjamins Publishing Company.

Kahn, R.L., Wolfe, D.M., Quinn, R.P., Snoek, J.D., & Rosenthal, R.A. (1964). Organizational stress: studies in role conflict and ambiguity. New York, USA: John Wiley.

King, L.A., & King, D.W. (1990) Role conflict and role ambiguity: A critical assessment of construct validty. Psychological Bulletin, 107(1), 48-64.

Kuckartz, U. (2014). Qualitative Text Analysis: A Guide to Methods, Practice & Using Software. London, UK: Sage Publications.

Mabry, E.A., & Barnes, R.E. (1980). The dynamics of small group communication. Englewood Cliffs, NJ: Prentice-Hall.

Maxwell, J.A., (1992). Understanding and validity in qualitative research. Harvard Educational Review, 62(3), 279-300.

McConnel, R. (1999). Inside the All Blacks: Behind the scenes with the world's most famous rugby team. London, UK: HarperCollins.

McGrath, J.E. (1984). Groups: Interaction and performance. Englewood Cliffs, NJ: Prentice Hall.

Salas, E. Dickinson,,T. L., Converse, S.A. and Tannenbaum, S. I.(1992). Toward an understanding of team performance and training. In R.W. Swezey & E. Salas (Eds.),

Teams: Their training and performance (pp.3-29). Norwood, NJ: Ablex

Shaw, M., and Costanzo, P. (1982). Theories of Social Psychology (2nd ed.). New York, USA: McGraw-Hill.

Sherif, M., & Sherif, C. W. (1953). Groups in Harmony and Tension. New York, USA: Harper & Brothers.

Van Sell, M., Brief, A. P., & Schuler, R. S. (1981). Role conflict and role ambiguity: Integration of the literature and directions for future research. Human Relations, 34, 43-71.

Weinberg, R.S., & Gould, D. (2011). Foundations of sport and exercise psychology (5th ed.). Champaign, IL: Human Kinetics.

A Turning Point for FPS Games

By Marc-André Messier

Over the past year or so, the major news in the FPS world didn't happen on the tournament field, but rather in the game creation department as this is when developers started cooking some brand new games for us, and possibly the tools for us to use in the future to compete. 2015 and 2016 saw the development of Unreal Tournament (which is often referred to as Unreal Tournament 4), a community-driven project that's already playable in pre-alpha for anyone who would want to join and ready for input from players. This process should bring the best out of the past and present for the series in terms of maps and game-play. You can already play even if the game hasn't been completed. Classic elements as well as new ones will be part of the final result, on top on the latest graphics.

This can be the start of a turning point for FPS games – big companies such as Epic Games finally willing to listen to just about anything the community wants. At least, the most loyal fans can be happy. However, is that really all there is to it to create the perfect eSports game? Are there more problems that have prevented FPS games from becoming the number one eSports games in terms of participation and viewership during the last 5 years?

Are open betas really the way to go?

However, while making such a game project community-driven like Unreal Tournament would seem like the missing gem to bringing back the popularity of FPS games, it seems like the formula has already been tried. Quake Live went a similar route when they made their free-to-play game available to anyone would want to put their hands on an early beta key, which really wasn't that hard back in 2009. The game then officially "released" in 2010 without much buzz, since pretty much everyone who wanted to play the game already had it. That's the problem with open betas – the show never really kicks off.

Much like Quake Live, this new Unreal Tournament could go under the radar and not bring in many players that would be new to the genre. The objective of FPS games should be to always bring in new players with something complete and easily accessible, and that's not something that open betas usually do really well. Unreal Tournament is currently in an open pre-alpha phase, and while a polished game and a release date are both priceless to bring in big numbers, this new title won't be going that route, which could end up hurting its buzz with no anticipation in the recipe. In the end, Quake Live could really serve as a lesson in eSports game creation and maybe that long open betas aren't the way to go to create buzz altogether. To compete with the new Unreal Tournament, the next Quake game will get a full release and date for us to patiently wait for.

Why not a clean and consistent visual style?

Quake by id Software is about ready to make a comeback as well and the name of the game will be Quake Champions. Contrarily to Quake Live, it's going to go for a darker visual style and it's to wonder if it's really going to fit the sports environment we're all trying to create. Quake Live did have this cool look for eSports and I liked the blue Intel-sponsored map (Bloodrun ZTN) that was presented at Quakecon 2016. That map looked much more exciting and professional than a dungeon. So we're letting go of the advantages of Quake Live as well? That's kind of disappointing. An eSports game needs to be consistent in its visual simplicity and straightforwardness for the player to enjoy it quickly both as a player and as a spectator. This is where the cleaner visual style of a game like Reflex by Turbo Pixels Studios, available as Early Access on Steam and also making its first steps in 2015-2016, could come in and steal the show to build the future FPS scene, but there's still a long way to go. Fortunately, Quake Champions is to focus on skill like mentioned in the first trailer video, and that's perhaps more important than visuals.

The issue with in-game menus and poor matchmaking

Then, one thing Quake Champions absolutely needs to fix is how we find our games, and more important-ly, how the newbies find their games. I haven't seen a Quake game so far that makes it quick and efficient for new players to find a game in a simple gametype and map setting. Eliminate all mods and confusion for the enjoyment of the newbie and then the genre might have some new hope. Matchmaking has to be quick and somehow we need to force people to start using it and enjoying it just like Starcraft. Too many options and you lose the player, and that's also true for the options you get within a game after it starts.

Quake needs to get on consoles

Next, I want to take on a little more of a controversial topic and it's the one to put Quake on consoles once again. My main argument would be that after trying out Quake Arena Arcade on Xbox Live, I was proven that fast-paced shooters can still be fun on consoles. It's simply a different way of proving your-self with your gaming skills. We've come to a point where the difference between mouse vs keyboard is understood and that we just want to enjoy a good game on our favorite platform.

But much more importantly, consoles bring in big sales numbers and if we're going to want as many spectators as we can for the show that Quake Champions can provide. There's something about PC that makes it a platform for the advanced user and that your average gamer simply won't like. I was therefore disappointed when I learned that Quake Champions would not be on consoles (and the same could be said about Unreal Tournament) since the general audience on console can't get all hyped up about the game like the PC gamers will.

The need for speed

While there's no need to turn gameplay speed all the way to Quake 3 CPMA Pro Mode style, there's certainly room for improvement on what was offered with Quake Live. Give quick players a little more room to dominate and the show will only get better. On the other hand, too much speed wouldn't give the spectator the time to appreciate the shots. I like when the players get the ability to dodge the logic of their opponents and dominate with superior speed and reflexes. Fortunately, Quake Champions looks to be quicker from the footage shown and that could only be good news. There are many elements that can amaze us in an FPS game, and no matter what the game chosen is for the big stage, we can't afford losing one in the process especially speed.

Overall, for this turning point to take place, there's going to need to be some commercial success or a shot straight to our hearts by putting a visually likeable game like Reflex in front of the audience because FPS games are seriously lagging behind the other eSports game in terms of numbers. Nothing feels like watching a close game of Quake on the big screen or maybe Unreal Tournament will end up having the last word by working with the gamers all the way throughout, but one thing is sure, we want to see results and big matches at the end of the day.

Marc-André Messier is a former professional gamer from Canada known as "4 Glory" who played in a variety of games. He notably placed 2nd at the 2007 CPL World Tour Finals for F.E.A.R. and played with top North American Call of Duty 2 team eGe. He's the author of the book Mindset: Travel with a Pro-Gamer available on Amazon and Kindle.

"Reverse-Gamification" Analysis of the Crowding-Out Effects in eSports

By Viktor Barie

In recent years Gamification has been given much attention in research. This can particularly be seen in the detailed literature review "Does Gamification Work? - A Literature Review of Empirical Studies on Gamification" (Hamari et al. 2014, p. 3029). Gamification can be briefly described with the goal of upgrading everyday activities with playful elements and thereby providing additional incentives. The aim of this study is whether the opposite is also possible. Can games be enriched with additional incentives by adding elements which are not usually associated with games? A professional career in a computer game may sound abstruse. Nevertheless, it has become an ever increasing topic and the development of eSports (electronic sports) shows that this is possible. This work examines possible effects on the motivation of players who now get paid to play.

Based on the theories of Crowding-Out and Gamification, the phenomenon of "Reverse Gamification" is introduced and investigated. Both theories are highly controversial. While the validity of the Crowding-Out theory is disputed (Frey & Jegen 2001a, p. 137), there is a variety of different views regarding Gamification. The result is that there are different approaches to the development and implementation (Deterding et al. 2011a; Huotari & Hamari 2011; Zichermann & Cunningham 2011). Within this work, the mentioned theories and their respective critique points are described. Following that, "Reverse Gamification" is first formulated in general in order to focus on the study of the Crowding-Out effects in eSports afterwards. The nature of this is especially tied to computer games. Therefore, Reverse Gamification is explained and considered in more detail specifically with regard to these. A questionnaire adds empirical results to the discussion. The relevance of Reverse Gamification for games which are not bound to computers is assumed but not further investigated.

To create the necessary background, the theories of Crowding-Out and Gamification will be analyzed. Crowding-Out is therefore introduced in chapter 2, beginning with intrinsic and extrinsic incentives as the backbones of the theory. Following that are the various manifestations of the theory and selected examples from the literature. Chapter 3 depicts a brief description of a few selected definitions of Gamification and chooses one of these as the basis for the remaining work. Then the goal of Gamification is considered and examined by using examples. In Chapter 4, Reverse Gamification will then be introduced based on the previously established theories. Specific examples with focus on the digital impact of Reverse Gamification follow. In regard to these, the relevance and the effects of Crowding-Out in eSports will be discussed. Chapter 5 presents an empirical study which tries to verify the assumptions made in the process. The structure of the questionnaire will be considered in more detail in order to check whether the theoretical foundations, laid out in chapter 4, have been complied with. This is followed by the statistical analysis and interpretation of the results. Chapter 6 concludes the findings of this work.

Crowding-Out

The idea of Crowding-Out arose in the 1970s by several authors at the same time. One of them is Titmuss with the book "The Gift Relationship" in which he describes the relationship between financial compensation and the subsequent stagnation of blood donations. A second origin of the term can be found in psychology. It has been discovered that monetary (external) rewards can undermine intrinsic motivation under certain conditions. While initially widespread rejection of the theory was practiced, in recent years more and more research has been conducted and has expanded its empirical significance. Meanwhile, the Crowding-Out effect, albeit still with little empirical relevance, is considered theoretically possible (Frey & Jegen 2001a, p. 132).

In the following chapters, first the individual components of the theory are introduced and its possible manifestations are enumerated and analyzed. Based on this, the Crowding-Out effects are then compared to the Relative-Price effect. This is done in regard to their impacts on an employer-employee relationship. Following that come illustrations of empirical studies and examples from literature.

Theory components

The main factors of the Crowding-Out theory are intrinsic and extrinsic motivation. Besides these, there is also the lack of motivation (demotivation). Figure 1 shows the various forms of motivation with their respective properties. These will now be examined in more detail.

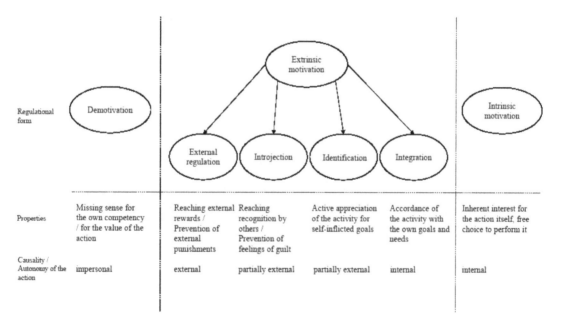

Figure 1: Forms of motivation and their respective properties. On the basis of Ryan & Deci (2001, p. 61).

Demotivation can be described as a state in which a person misses any intention to do something. This lack of intention can have many reasons. The person could for example plainly see no value in the action or otherwise not feel competent enough to perform the task well enough (Ryan & Deci 2001, p. 61).

Intrinsic motivation has its origins in incentives that come from the person himself. The reward for completing the activity is the activity itself and the fun and/or the satisfaction that results from carrying out the activity. Indicators are therefore the free choice to perform a certain activity, the inherent interest in it and the resulting pleasure. Accordingly, studies that try to demonstrate existing intrinsic motivation focus on precisely these indicators (Ryan & Deci 2001, p. 57).

Contrary to intrinsic motivation, extrinsic motivation stirs from the fact that a certain result is achieved through the activity. The activity itself is differentiated from the incentive to carry it out. The desired result may be for example recognition, perfection and financial rewards. The form of extrinsic motivation can vary greatly. This variation is particularly due to the type of autonomy when performing the activity. There is a difference between a person aiming to excellence in a specific activity and the person being forced to perform it. According to Ryan & Deci, there are four different forms of extrinsic motivation, each form having a different type of autonomy coming with it. The form with the least autonomy is the external regulation. It is the original form of extrinsic motivation and the associated activities are characterized by strictly external influence. This may be being forced to do it or to reach a certain reward (or to work around a specific punishment). The next form is the introjected regulation, which involves foreign expectations into the own actions. These actions are usually carried out in order to escape guilt or to strengthen the self-confidence. Regulation by identification with an activity is the next stage of extrinsic motivation. The performing person has recognized the value of the action and accepts it as such, even if it is not necessarily fun or interesting (and is therefore not intrinsically motivating). The last form is the regulation through integration. Through the incorporation of the activity and its benefits into the own understanding of valuable activities results in the highest level of autonomy - free will. However, there can be no talk of intrinsic motivation as there continues to be a reason to perform the activity for a greater good, and not for the activity itself and its interesting properties (Ryan & Deci 2001, pp. 60-62). Nonetheless, especially the latter two forms of extrinsic motivation are similar to intrinsic motivation and cannot be distinguished accurately. The transition is smooth and is therefore not clearly determinable.

The Crowding-Out theory refers to the influence of extrinsic incentives to intrinsic motivation. There are different versions (Frey & Jegen 2001a, p. 134.):

- Adventitious extrinsic incentives reduce existing intrinsic motivation (crowding-out).
- Adventitious extrinsic incentives increase the existing intrinsic motivation (crowding-in).
- Adventitious extrinsic incentives do not affect the existing intrinsic motivation.

In order that one of these can occur, it must be given that intrinsic motivation was present from the outset (Frey & Jegen 2000, p.10).

Considering the psychological aspect, there are two special causes of crowding effects. These are damages to the self-determination and self-confidence. Suppose a person is intrinsically motivated to perform an activity and does so without significant interference by others. Then adventitious external control measures take place regarding if and how the person performs the activity. It is now possible that the intrinsic motivation of the person changes to extrinsic motivation due to the change of autonomy and therefore harms the self-determination. This varies depending on the degree of self-determination in the activity and the relation of intrinsic incentives to extrinsic control. If the intrinsic motivation of a person is not valued, the self-confidence will be damaged and the effort going into the activity may decrease (Frey & Jegen 2001a, p. 136).

These causes of crowding effects can now cause the following situations (Frey & Jegen 2001a, p. 137):

- Crowding-out may occur, if external interference damages the self-determination and self-confidence. This happens especially if the experienced interference shifts outside of the own control area.
- Crowding-in may occur, if the external interference is perceived as supportive action. Thus, the self-determination and self-confidence may increase and intrinsic motivation is enhanced.

Below, the Crowding-Out theory is put into the context of the Relative-Price Theory.

Crowding-Out- and Relative-Price-Effects

While the above scenarios merely depict a general activity, they can of course also occur within an employer-employee relationship. In such situations, the adventitious extrinsic incentives are often in monetary form. This may then cause qualitative or quantitative changes of the work performance due to decreasing or increasing intrinsic motivation of the employee. These changes can be of positive or negative nature, which contradicts the traditional Relative-Price theory. It formulates the relationship, in which increased financial incentives result in increased work performances. Accordingly, this effect is based entirely on extrinsic motivation and ignores the effects on the intrinsic aspect. Instead, it is considered as a given constant which does not change (Frey & Jegen 2001b, p. 591).

By analyzing an extrinsic interference while taking the Relative-Price and Crowding-Out effects into account, three different situations may arise (Frey & Jegen 2001b, p. 593):

- The relative-price effect takes places and the work performance increases with increasing extrinsic incentives. The work performance would also rise, if the intrinsic motivation is reinforced by the increased extrinsic incentives (a crowding-in effect occurs). Thus the difference between crowding-in and relative-price effect is not the outcome, but rather the cause of it.
- The crowding-out effect takes place and the external interference harms the intrinsic motivation. Accordingly, a reduction of work performance results through the decreasing intrinsic motivation. However, this can only be true under the assumption, that disciplinary measures have no or only insufficient effect.
- Both effects can occur and therefore an external interference may have both positive and negative effects on the work performance. Which of these effects is stronger depends on the situation and the type of interference must be adjusted accordingly.

Which of the three situations the employment relationship is prevalent should be found out before an external interference in order to better assess its consequences. This of course is not always possible. Furthermore, an employment relationship cannot be accurately represented in such a simplified form. Nevertheless, the various interdependencies may very well be observed on the basis of those.

A prominent example are parents at daycare centers, who come too late to collect their children. As the supervisors thereby have to work longer, it is natural to do something about it. A typical economic approach would now introduce a financial penalty, which will have the parents to pay a certain fee when they late. The expectation is that the parents try to be on time the next time. To test this, an experiment was conducted in an Israeli kindergarten. First, late coming parents were noted over a certain time period. At some time, a penalty was introduced and the number of latecomers was again written down. The outcome was a significant increase of latecomers compared to the time without a punishment. Even after the punishment was removed, the number of late coming parents has remained at the higher level. This can be explained using the Crowding-Out theory. The introduction of the punishment reduced, if not eliminated entirely, the intrinsic motivation to be on time. The non-financial relationship between parents and caregivers turned into a financial relationship. Thereby the payable penalty was now considered as a price for which the children can stay longer in the daycare center. As you can see, the opposite of what was initially sought can occur due to insufficient consideration of crowding effects (Frey & Jegen 2001b, p. 602).

In addition to this and other similar examples, there are also experiments that clearly show the existence and also its significance of crowding effects. The following examines the experiments of Deci more closely (Deci 1971, p. 108-115). The hypotheses in his experiments are as follows:

A person is involved with an activity because of intrinsic motivation. Now adventitious extrinsic incentives are added in form of monetary compensation. It may

- reduce the intrinsic motivation to continue the activity. (Hypothesis 1)
- increase the intrinsic motivation to continue the activity. (Hypothesis 2)
- not change the intrinsic motivation at all. (Null hypothesis)

The conducted experiments are all similar to each other. In three phases, test subjects had to perform a specific task. In the present case this was a puzzle which was widespread among the students at the time and therefore intrinsic motivation to tackle the puzzle was assumed.

There was each a control group and an experimental group. The control group had the same test environment, without any extrinsic influence at every phase. In the experimental group, the experiment was constructed as follows: In the first phase, the activity itself was to be done. In the second phase, extrinsic incentives were added. In one of the experiments, it was monetary reward which depended on performance. In another experiment, extrinsic incentives were given in the form of recognition, not considering the performance at all. If a test subject did not cope with the activity, it was told that this was a hard-on issue or has been dissolved by virtually no one. In the third phase the extrinsic incentives have been removed for all experiments. Furthermore, there was a ten minute break between the phases in which the subject has been granted clearance to spend the time as it wished (they were offered other activities, such as an extensive journal supply). Within these pauses, the subject was unbeknownst observed how much time is spend on the puzzle regardless. The following observations with respect to the experimental groups in comparison to the control groups were identified:

In the experiment with financial reward motivation increased during the second phase. This suggests that extrinsic incentives can initially increase the overall motivation. In the third phase where extrinsic incentives have been removed, the observed motivation / work performance plummeted far below the measured value of the first phase. This suggests that the extrinsic incentive indeed increases motivation in the short term. However, the intrinsic motivation suffers respectively and a crowding-out occurs. This clearly points towards the validity of hypothesis 1.

In the experiment, in which the extrinsic incentives were created in through positive feedback, it was observed that the motivation in the control group has been steadily declining throughout the phases. In the experimental group, however, occurred an increase in motivation during phase 2 while it was back on the level of the first phase during the last phase. So while the motivation steadily decreased in the control group, the experimental group had a short influx and then maintained its original motivation at the end of the experiment. While this may not constitute direct evidence, it still tends to favor hypothesis 2. Therefore it can be assumed, that adventitious extrinsic incentives in the form of positive feedback enhances intrinsic motivation, or at least does not lower it.

However, it should be mentioned that the presented experiments do not have absolute expressiveness. While many hedge measures have been taken to keep random errors and deviations small, their existence cannot be excluded in the experiments. Nevertheless, it can be assumed that the experiments carried out suggest the validity of the hypotheses 1 and 2.

The presented experiments were conducted and evaluated in many varieties by different researchers. Overall, similar results to the ones here presented were identified. A good overview offer Deci, Koestner & Ryan with a meta-analysis of 128 experiments on the effects of extrinsic rewards (Deci et al. 1999, p. 627-668).

Gamification

Gamification is a term which has received no uniform definition up until to the present state of research. Researchers disagree over the purpose and use, which can especially be seen in a debate between Zichermann and Deterding, which began with a sharp critique towards the book "Gamification by Design" (Deterding 2011; Zichermann & Cunningham 2011).

The concept of Gamification itself is rather old, while the respective term emerged in the 21st century. However, it cannot be said for sure when the word "Gamification" was coined for the first time. The sources agree that the interest and research regarding Gamification have risen sharply only after 2010 (Hamari et al., 2014, p. 3025). Designations such as "productivity games", "funware", "playful design" and many more have also been introduced. Gamification however has established itself as the leading term (Deterding et al. 2011a, p. 9).

Definitions

In recent years there have been several research papers, which tried to give the imprecise term some substance and empirical evidence. The main findings and defining elements will be processed in the following chapter.

Hamari & Huotari see gamification as a bundling of the core service with additional benefits. These take forms such as feedback and interaction mechanisms in order to increase the overall value of the user. Within this definition, any system can be coupled with Gamification, even games themselves (Huotari &

Hamari 2011, p. 1).

Zichermann views Gamification from a marketing oriented approach. This can be seen in the introduction to his book "Gamification by Design":

"What do Foursquare, Zynga, Nike+, and Groupon have in common? These and many other brands use gamification to deliver a sticky, viral, and engaging experience for their customers. [...] Whether you're an executive, developer, producer, or product specialist, Gamification by Design will show you how game mechanics can help you build customer loyalty" (Zichermann & Cunningham 2011, Abstract).

Zichermann relates Gamification specifically to the generation and maintenance of customer loyalty. Therefore, he focuses in particular on services which aim lies on such effects. One example is payback points: A virtual currency, of which the customer does not know the exact value but still assess it as lucrative (Zichermann & Cunningham 2011, p. 7).

In the course of this work, the definition of Deterding is considered in more detail, which can be paraphrased as follows:

"Gamification is the use of elements which are characteristic for the design of games. This takes place in contexts which do not lie in a gaming environment" (Deterding et al. 2011a, p. 13).

The choice fell onto this definition, as it is limiting regarding to the possible forms of Gamification while at the same time not being so specific so that it allows Gamification to be used in many application areas. Furthermore, it has been developed and researched in the scientific sense.

Definition components according to Deterding

The individual components of the definition are: Games, elements, design and context of a non-gaming environment.

There is distinct difference between playing and gaming. Playing is an activity without clear goals. The focus therefore lies on the activity itself and the experience coming from it. Games, however, have clear rules and structures. In a game, one has to achieve a certain goal and often times there is a competitive aspect involved. It is also about the quality of results and less about the experience while playing. Gamification refers mostly, as the name suggests, to the gaming aspect (Deterding et al. 2011a, p. 11). It does not mean that playing aspects can be totally ignored. However, the focus is on the rule-based and goal-oriented games. The character of an activity that is enriched with Gamification can also depend on the eye of the beholder. The one monitoring the activity can have the gaming aspect in focus and accordingly sets a value on the results of the process. The person who performs the activity, however, may be only interested in the process itself. The results are provided only as a by-product and are not important to the person. The elements used in Gamification should be characteristic for games. The question here, however, is: When is an item a unique characteristic for a game? That's just answerable in a nonspecific way. The elements should appear in many games, are associated with these and be important for its game mechanics (Deterding et al. 2011a, p. 12). This is formulated in a very open manner and leaves space for interpretation. This means that not always because something is called Gamification, it is Gamification for real. It is also not easy to distinguish whether an application is enriched by Gamification using game elements or if it just is a game itself. Among other things, it depends on the user: Does he play (gaming) the application or does he use it? This distinction is always subjectively made and is furthermore subject to social influence (Deterding et al. 2011a, pp. 11-12).

Gamification uses game design elements. Such elements have different levels of abstraction. These range from design choices regarding the interface to the used methods (such as the incentive systems within a game). The implementation, however, is the realization of these design decisions. This can be achieved in many different ways and is therefore not characterized as a design element (Deterding et al.,2011a, p. 12).

The non-gaming environment is particularly important in Gamification. If that is not given, one rather speaks about "serious games". These are full-fledged games that aim to convey specific content (Deterding et al. 2011a, p. 11). Such content may be improving motoric skills or memorizing historical data. Another point is that the accumulation of a game with further game design elements only is game design itself, and not Gamification (Deterding et al. 2011a, p. 12). The required non-game environments can occur in many forms. Just as there are training games, health games and news games, there can also be applications for training, health and news that are enriched with Gamification (Deterding et al. 2011a, p. 12). This can be illustrated using the example of a football training: The trainer wants to improve the endurance of his players. In order to achieve this, he can construct a game in which continuous running leads into a strategic advantage. Therefore, it strengthens the endurance by playing the game (a serious game in the form of a training game). He can also enhance the endurance training with game elements. For example, the players who voluntarily run laps after training can acquire free drinks at the bar. This can be done by acquiring points for the laps and various drinks cost a different amount of points. Thus, the coach made endurance training interesting by introducing game elements.

The Goal of Gamification

Generally speaking, Gamification is a collective term for systems that are designed to cause improvements of user experience and their commitment to the activity. These systems are in contexts that do not take place in a game, but in everyday situations such as in work and recreational environments (Deterding et al. 2011b, p. 2425).

The idea is to use the elements of a game which encourages the user to start the game and continue to spend time on it. So why does one play? In the foreground lies the fun itself, but crucial factors are also the challenges, long-term motivators and social aspects of a game. Thus, elements that provide playful, entertaining and challenging experiences are integrated into the activity (Deterding et al. 2011a, p. 11).

Therefore, it is the goal of Gamification to enrich an activity with other incentives. Ideally, not only the general level of motivation, but the intrinsic motivation in particular should increase that way. This would be a crowding-in effect. If no crowding-in applies, it should at least not cause a crow-ding-out. As it is known from the previous chapter, the correct use of the crowding effects is not a trivial matter. Everyone approaches an activity and the associated incentives differently. Subsequently, everyone reacts differently to extrinsic interference as well. The effects of Gamification further depend on the structure and nature of the activity. Introducing a points system in an environment where diligent work habits are a must does not necessarily make as sense as in an environment where speed matters most (for example conceptual work compared to retail). Whether Gamification leads to the desired purpose cannot be predicted with certainty.

In Deterdings "Six Invitations to Rethink Gamification" (Deterding 2014) are six points listed which indicate the necessity to reconsider Gamification. The need for improvement in the definition and implementation of Gamification is addressed. Deterding further puts emphasis on the necessity to have to think and act outside the narrow and context-free structure. In order for Gamification not to miss its intentions, the environment of the action needs to be taken into consideration. The environment consists of ethic and social aspects, personal attitude of the user and other environmental conditions (Deterding 2014, pp. 307-326).

A functioning system in Europe can fail completely when used in Asia, a non-functioning system in Germany can provide revolutionary results in France. Even within the same region and the same employment sector, a firm A can fail with applying a Gamification measure while firm B succeeds and increases the work performance by 200%. The overall system of the application needs to allude the individual user.

Examples for Gamification

Examples for Gamification can be found in large quantities. The following examines two of them in more detail.

"Stack Overflow is a question and answer site for professionals and enthusiast programmers" (Stack exchange inc 2015). Any question regarding a programming problem can expect to get a constructive response, if it was sufficiently detailed and related to practice. The questions and answers can be rated by users. These evaluations then form the basis for the reputation of a user which depicts the general usefulness for the community. In addition, there are badges for certain milestones of a user. Such milestones are for example a certain number of high-quality responses or evaluations of other response. Grant and Betts have investigated the effect of such a system. They came to the conclusion, that while not all users are affected, there is still an indication for a trend. Users who are nearing the completion of a particular badge tend to spend more time on that particular task to achieve the badge. Immediately after the acquisition, the corresponding activity is neglected again. However, the resulting responses and evaluations remain available(Grant & Betts 2013, p. 65-68).

But why does it work? Why should users carry out work related tasks, just because they are lured with something that apparently does not bring any value with it? The most important point seems to be that the users show interest for the topic on their own. They are intrinsically motivated to seek a challenge from the questions and therefore want to find a solution. Furthermore, the site provides assistance for their own problems as well. But this can only be done under the premise that enough users are providing the necessary content. The solution to their own problems either already exist or can be developed interactively in collaboration with other users. The now adventitious virtual values such as reputation and badges are an additional incentive to carry out these activities. They might also bring individual users to focus on an area that they so far neglected. The virtual values then get a real benefit within the community. A user can compare badges and achievements with other users. The social aspect is therefore also an important factor (Grant & Betts 2013, p. 65-68).

Another example is the Microsoft Language Quality game. In this "game", the focus lies on the many different languages in every possible dialogue window. In order to diminish the resource usage, employees around the world were addressed to assist with the quality management of dialogues in Windows 7.

The assistance was furthermore outside of the regular working hours. As an incentive to still participate, the employees were given points for each recognized error. These points were then noted on regional and international rankings. A lot of employees saw it as a competition with offices around the world and perceived the process as entertaining and challenging. Not only the personal success was important, but also for the branch to be as high as possible on the international leaderboard was pursued. The goal was to win (Werbach & Hunter 2012, p. 18).

Reverse-Gamification

The study around Reverse-Gamification is based on the theories of Gamification and Crowding-Out. While Gamification focuses on non-gaming environments, Reverse-Gamification does the opposite and focuses on crowding effects which may appear in gaming environments. Further investigations rest upon the following assumption, which is based on Deterdings definition of Gamification:

Reverse-Gamification is the use of elements which are characteristic for the design of subjects not associated with games. This takes place in contexts which are in a gaming environment.

The elements used in Reverse-Gamification should be characteristic of subjects that are not associated with games. Since this description is very open and difficult to specify, the characteristic elements of such one subject must be identified first. However, the elements should occur in many variations of the same type of subject and they should be important for its construction. Accordingly, the design of these elements should be viewed similarly differentiated. The design depends on the specific activity of which the characteristic elements are to be integrated.

The component regarding subjects which are not associated with games is the first big difference to the definition of Gamification. As the description implies, every potential context is included as long as is not a game. Whether something is a game or not must be distinguished from case to case and is furthermore open for discussion. The context of the game environment is the second big difference to Gamification. However, Reverse-Gamification also emphasizes the gaming aspect more so than the playing aspect. The aforementioned serious games constitute a subcategory of Reverse-Gamification. They are full-fledged games that do not aim to just entertain.

The goal of a game with Reverse-Gamification depends on the specific game itself. Such a game is not necessarily enriched with non-gaming elements on purpose. Therefore, its goal is not always determinable. It may develop over time. The game itself remains playful, entertaining and brings challenging experiences along with it. Apart from that, the objectives of other subjects are transferred to the game itself. Figure 2 shows the defining differences between Gamification and Reverse-Gamification.

Gamification		Reverse-Gamification	
Definition component	Example	Definition component	Example
Non-game context	Service provider, who tries to sell a product	Game context	Playing a computer game
Elements (characteristic for games)	Ladderboards, achievements	Elements (characteristic for games)	Financial rewards, keeping a schedule
Design (of the elements)	Gettin provision based on sales quantitiy, reaching milestones of the firm	Design (of the elements)	Streaming, participating in tournaments, advertising revenue
Possible goals	Increasing the motivation of a salesperson to make more sales, overall increase in sales	Possible goals	Making a living, having fun

Figure 2: Comparison of Gamification and Reverse-Gamification

Examples for Reverse-Gamification

A prominent example of Crowding-Out is the child who regularly mows the lawn (Deci 1971, p. 105). The child finds pleasure in the activity and continues to do so voluntarily. One day the parents decide that the child should receive a monetary reward. Now what happens to the intrinsic motivation of the child? The child could feel compelled to mow the lawn and thus loses his inner drive to do it voluntarily. The child could just as well mow the lawn with more motivation, because he sees the importance of its activities in a different light. Or the reward was limited for a specific time period. The child may then refuse to continue the work without receiving a reward for it. Whether and in what way the intrinsic and extrinsic incentives change depends on the child. Transferring the example into the context of Reverse-Gamification could look like the following:

The child wants to play in the garden. The parents want to encourage that and offer a reward. The child now does not feel the urge to play anymore, but as it gets a reward for it, it continues to play either way. The reward is now the main incentives to further pursue the game and the initial intrinsic motivation was crowded-out by the extrinsic incentive. The other way around is also possible. A game, for which the child has peaked an interest, now receives additional incentives. The game may now become even more interesting and might be so for a longer time period as if it had no reward attached to it.

Design elements of non-gaming subjects can be simulations of real markets or even work related tasks. The mind wanders to the numerous auction houses within popular games like World of Warcraft (Blizzard Entertainment 2004) and Eve Online (CCP Games 2003). But even game platforms like Steam (Valve Corporation 2003) have their so-called Market Place, whereupon virtual items are sold by players for players. The value of such items can be a massive sum in form of game currency. High amounts of real currency are also not uncommon anymore. In 2005, the company "Itembay" made $ 300 million in sales acting as a broker of virtual items. This is comparable to the sales of game developer companies such as NCSoft (Huhh 2006, p. 2). Another example is the gold farming phenomenon, in which players accumulate large amounts of virtual currency of a game (oftentimes gold) in order to interchange it for real money outside the game (Heeks 2010, p. 6).

The main focus of this work lies on eSports, which represents a big part of Reverse-Gamification and can be described with the following work thesis:

ESports includes playing computer or console games to a degree in which the player can partly or wholly finance his livelihood.

Within the study, two types of players can be distinguished:

- Players, who mainly broadcast their activities on streaming platforms in order to finance their livelihood. This is mostly achieved by advertising revenues, donations from viewers and corporate sponsorship (Pro-Streamer).
- Players, who are under contract from an organization to play at the highest level of competition for prestige and prize money (Pro-Gamer).

It should be noted that these two groups are not necessarily mutually exclusive. A Pro-Streamer may as well have Pro-Gamer aspects and vice versa. A good example is Jeffrey Shih, a professional hearthstone player, who made streaming his profession and also participates in many tournaments with financial winnings.

Empirical Study

This chapter covers the questionnaire and its hypotheses. It examines the effects of adventitious extrinsic incentives on existing intrinsic incentives. The main question is the following:

Is it possible to enrich (computer) games with (work) elements to thereby provide the game with additional incentives which normally are not associated with games?

The hypotheses are divided into the two main objects of the study – Crowding-Out and Reverse-Gamification. Hypothesis H0C refers to Crowding-Out: "Extrinsic incentives do not affect the intrinsic incentives in eSports". The rival hypothesis H1C is formulated as follows: "Extrinsic incentives affect the intrinsic incentives in eSports, namely (H1aC) positively (crowding-in) or (H1bC) negatively (crowding-out)".

The hypothesis H0R regarding Reverse-Gamification is "E-athletes do not see their current life stage as a profession." The corresponding rival hypothesis H1R therefore is: "E-athletes see their current stage of life as a profession."

Factors for the Crowding-Out hypotheses are the changes in intrinsic and extrinsic incentives. For Reverse-Gamification, the factors are the expenditure of time, reasons for playing and their attitude towards playing.

Questionnaire structure

The examination method is an online questionnaire, which consists of six sections. The survey can be found und appendix B. The first two sections represent the introduction, wherein the first part defines the approximate theme and the target group of the survey. The second section requests demographic information, such as age, gender and whether the respondent would see itself as pro-gamer or pro-streamer. Their main game and other games are also requested. The main game would be the game which the respondent streams the most or for which he is paid to play.

The main part of the questionnaire includes sections three to five with each section containing a secluded issue for themselves. The third section deals with the time before the respondent pursued their current activity. It mainly serves for gathering reference values regarding existing intrinsic motivation. These values apply to the reasons of playing, the fun level and the time spend dealing with the main game and other games, as well as the intention to launch an eSports career. They also serve as a first approximation to the phenomenon of Reverse-Gamification. Section four refers to the current situation of the respondent and contains an analogous representation of questions. Sections three and four test the abovementioned individual factors of the hypotheses. Section five asks for the specific assessments regarding the hypotheses from the respondents. The final section of the questionnaire includes information about the study.

Evaluation

Over 350 people were contacted personally via social networks. 37 of these completed the questionnaire and could be used for the evaluation. Thus, the return rate is roughly 10%. Due to the relatively small sample line, the following evaluations have only limited significance. However, a larger survey could not be done because of the limitations of the bachelor thesis. Nevertheless, tendencies towards the validity of the hypotheses can still be disputed.

Statistical analysis

The demographical distribution is as follow. 83.8% of the respondents are male, 16.2% are female. The age ranges from 16 to 29, wherein 62.1% lies between 20 and 23. These observations are generally comparable to the actual distribution in the population, while the female proportion may be a bit over-represented. The geographical distribution is highly influenced by linguistic barriers and is thus largely confined to the western continents. 37.8% have completed their school education with no further degrees. 35.1% are either currently studying or discontinued their studies. Some have a university degree, but these show to be the exception. 81.1% call themselves pro-gamers, 18.9% consider themselves pro-streamers. This is partly because pro-gamers were easier to reach out to, as they were listed on their respective team website. Pro-streamers are generally less present in such listings and needed closer scrutiny whether they corresponded to the target group or not.

Next is the evaluation of the time period before the respondents became pro-gamers / pro-streamers. As expected, the reasons for playing were mostly the fun itself (94.5% checked this option). But distraction (32.4%), pastime (29.7%), being in company (18.9%) and the plan to become a pro-gamer / pro-streamer (37.8%) were also checked. By specifying the possible answers, their answers got limited and might have been affected. However, that was necessary since otherwise no sufficient comparison could have been made. The preset choices were selected as neutral as possible. 37.8% perceived very much fun, 29.7% much fun, 24.3% moderate fun and 8.1% perceived only little fun. Approximately 6 hours were spent on the main game and about 2.5 hours on side games on average. The union of the two tables gives a precise distribution of hours per respondent and can be looked up in the appendix. 56.8% of respondents perceived the playing more or less as a kind of compensation from real life, 27% denied this statement.

For the time period in which the respondents already were pro-gamer / pro-streamer, the following observations can be made. The stated reasons for playing the main game are mostly fun (62.2%), training (59.5%) and financial income (62.2%). Other reasons were: distraction, pastime, being in company, social recognition and being bound to a contract. Reasons cited for playing other games amounts mainly on fun (83.8%), distraction (27.0%), pastime (37.7%) and being in company (27.0%). Figure 3 depicts the differences of the two time periods. While previously almost all respondents played mostly for fun, the amount of those who called fun than main reason decreased by 32.6%. However, it must be noted that the reasons training and financial income were not offered during the preceding phase.

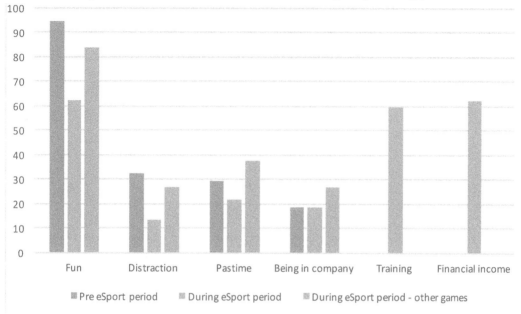

Figure 3: Comparison of the reasons for playing. Values in percentages of all respondents.

The perceived fun while playing the main game during the eSport period was for 18.9% of the participants very high, for 27.0% high, for 40.5% moderate and for 13.5% low. Comparing that to the pre eSport period (see Figure 4), it is apparent that the associated fun was higher while the respondents were not a pro-gamer / pro-streamer. The majority has changed from "Very fun" to "Moderately fun". Predominant reasons included the perceived coercion to earn financial income (45.9%) and that the lengthy occupation with the game reduced the associated enjoyment. Other reasons were for example: "You can no longer play for fun, only play competitively to get better" and "Less fun, more satisfying though" . Only one person had more fun with the main game during the eSport time than before with all games together. The remainder perceived either the same or less fun. The expenditure of time per day shifted to seven hours for the main game and two hours for other games. This means a small shift in the distribution towards the main game. The question if other games pose a form of compensation activity gave the following results: 43.2% voted rather yes, 32.4% rejected this statement. No trend is recognizable by comparing the result to the previous question regarding the compensation activity. Of the people who stream (81.1%), 60.0% play computer games very often even if they do not stream at that point of time. 26.6% sometimes play outside of the stream and 6.7% play almost never off-stream. The last 6.7% always have their stream on whenever they play something. Although 62.2% of respondents have a stream or training schedule, 40.5% of those do not strictly implement it. The remaining 37.8% have no schedule at all.

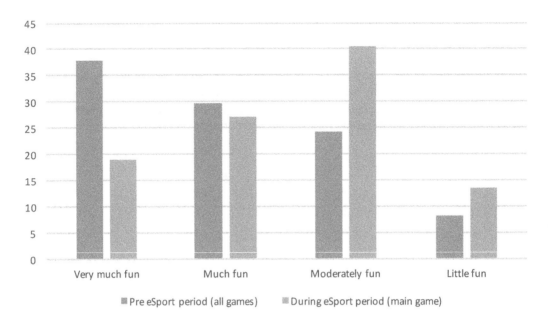

Figure 4: Fun while playing. Values in percentage of all respondents.

Following that, the respondents were asked for their personal opinion on certain areas. Only 5.4% have stated a reduction in their motivation. 29.7% reported a strong, 35.1% reported a slight increase. 29.7% said that their motivation has not changed. Figure 5 shows contrasting juxtaposition of the change of motivation and change of fun. It is displayed on a scale of -2 to +2. -2 stands for a strong negative change, +2 for a strong positive change and 0 represents no change. While the variation of the motivation was queried directly, the change of fun was based on a comparison of the previous statements. Generally it can be seen that the motivation has increased in general, but the fun while playing either remained the same or decreased. However, there is also a non-negligible amount that has no change of the two values. 40.5% indicated that they would play the game as before, even if they would not receive any financial income anymore, 40.5% would play it less. The remaining 19.0% would practically stop playing the game at all. The answers regarding the current phase of their life can be seen in Figure 6 and are predominantly of vocational nature. The sources of income are mostly through their respective eSport organizations (70.3%), stream revenues such as advertising and donations (35.1%) and sponsorships (21.6%). Tournament winnings have also been mentioned several times (18.9%).

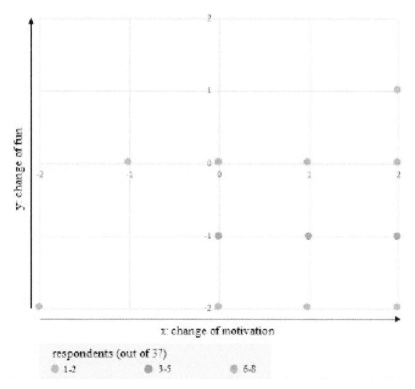

Figure 5: Change of motivation and fun.

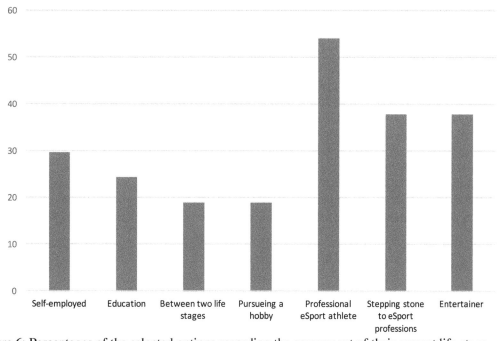

Figure 6: Percentages of the selected options regarding the assessment of their current life stage.

Interpretation of the results

Based on the high percentage of respondents selecting fun as the main incentive for playing computer games (before the eSports period), it can be assumed that intrinsic motivation was present from the outset. Distraction, pastime and being in company also commends that the respondents were interested on their own initiative. The perceived fun while playing is predominantly high or very high, which is another indication of pre-existing intrinsic motivation. After extrinsic incentives have been added during the eSports period (mostly in the form of financial compensation), fun is still one of the main underlying reasons for playing the main game. However, 32.3% of respondents no longer selected fun as a reason anymore, while training and financial income emerged as more significant reasons. The perceived fun on the main game was not as distinct in comparison. Figure 5-3 shows an interesting development of change of motivation in comparison to the change of fun. Besides two runaway values at (-2, -2) and (0, -1), there is a discernible trend regarding an overall increase or stable motivation while the fun predominantly decreased or remained stable. Most respondents can be found on the x-axis (an orange dot means that 6-8 respondents are on the respective coordinates). Another factor is the decrease of readiness to play the game, if the financial income would no longer be present.

The observations suggest a loss of intrinsic motivation while extrinsic motivation has increased. This depicts a tendency towards hypothesis H1bC. Specifically, the observation of increasing motivation at the same time with decreasing fun suggests a crowding-out. However, the stated reasons (such as the previously mentioned comment "Less fun, more satisfying though.") leave room for the possibility that intrinsic motivation is not crowded-out, but has merely been shifted. The agglomeration of stable fun also indicates hypotheses H0C and H1aC. As the concrete reason for the decrease of motivation is not known, it can point towards an increase of intrinsic motivation (H1aC) or towards indifference (H0C). The influence of extrinsic incentives on intrinsic motivation is therefore not generally applicable and different persons may give different results because of their different traits. Which development is dominant depends on the individual person, as it was already assumed for Crowding-Out on its own. Based on these observations can the relevance of the Crowding-Out theory regarding eSports be assumed.

The time spend for the main game has risen from an average of 6 hours per day to an average of 7 hours per day. The time spend for other games has dropped from 2.5 to 2 hours on average. So there is only a slight shift towards the main game. However, that may be because the overall time of the day was already exhausted and greater customization of the allocated time was not available as such. Based on the added reasons training and financial income, which each were selected by circa 60% of respondents, a tendency can be observed which suggests a work setting to the activity. This tendency is supported by the answers regarding the assessment of their particular life stage, which have been mostly of vocational nature. Therefore it can be assumed that the activity is generally seen more as profession rather than as a hobby. Thus, there is a tendency to hypothesis H1R ("E-athletes see their stage of life as a professional."). However, an unambiguous statement for the hypotheses of Reverse-Gamification is not possible.

Credibility analysis

The questions should uphold certain quality criteria: objectivity, reliability and validity. The objectivity criterion states the independency of the results in reference to the experiment conductor. Reliability refers to the reproducibility of the results. Validity is the verification whether the experiment measures what it is supposed to measure (Homburg 2014, pp. 253-254). Furthermore, the question should be easy, neutral and unambiguous (Homburg 2014, p. 314).

The objectivity criterion of the questionnaire is partly given. The answers of the participants are free from the influence of the conductor due to it being an online survey. However, it cannot be excluded that the evaluation and interpretation of the answers may have subjective leeway due to the lack of comparisons with similar surveys. Because of the relatively small number of participants, the reliability is not clearly determined as deviations and random errors cannot be precisely identified. The validity of the questions cannot be guaranteed either, since the questionnaire is designed explorative. Lastly, the small number of participants results in a limited significance of the results. However, as the questionnaire was part of the bachelor thesis, there were no further resources to conduct a bigger research.

Simplicity, neutrality and clarity was paid attention to during the pretest of the questionnaire and discrepancies have been taken care of. Some questions, however, violate the neutrality aspect. Possible answers were given in order to be able to evaluate the answers. Nevertheless, these question still provided the option to provide individualized input. Due to the partial compliance with the quality criteria, the evaluation of the questionnaire needs to be treated with caution. Nonetheless, it is assumed that the obtained results give a good impression of the situation and fulfill their purpose in the scope of this work.

Summary

Gamification aims to bring playful, entertaining and challenging experiences into activities. These activities are in non-game context environments. This is achieved by adding game design elements which affects the intrinsic and extrinsic incentives of the people involved. Desirable is a positive change in motivation. However, the Crowding-Out effects may also impact the motivation negatively. Possible effects are crowding-out (extrinsic incentives replace intrinsic motivation), crowding-in (intrinsic motivation gets reinforced through extrinsic incentives) and no change in the intrinsic incentives. All environmental conditions must be observed in order to obtain the desired result.

Reverse-Gamification is a phenomenon contrary to Gamification. It is the use of elements within a game context, which are characteristic of subjects not related to games. This may have been the intention of the game either from the outset (as for example in serious games) or the game adopts such elements in retrospect. The goal of a game enriched with Reverse-Gamification is not generally determinable and depends on the individual case. It may already be set in stone, evolve during the process or even be insignificant. The focus of the work is whether it is possible to enrich games with non-game elements, so that these receive adventitious extrinsic incentives. Is an example of a theoretical construct was created in which this could be the case. Concrete examples were kept within the general context of computer games and eSports. Furthermore, an empirical study got conducted in order to research these effects. Observations showed that eSports have tendencies to contain crowding effects. Furthermore, it seems that crowding-out is more prominent than crowding-in. Which effect and to what extent depends on the individual person. In addition, the respondents showed a change of attitude towards the activity. After the computer game was pursued professionally, it was no longer regarded as just a hobby but also as a professional activity. The perceived fun continues to play a role, however, it is no longer the main reason to keep playing the game.

A more specific study of the formulation of Reverse-Gamification is indispensable. However, it was not possible to do so within the scope of this work and was therefore not pursued. Furthermore, it only examined the effects of Reverse-Gamification in eSports. Future work regarding Reverse-Gamification could set the focus onto the precise specification of the definition. An observation of the phenomenon in a wider context, especially concerning games which do not occur on a computer, is also is also of interest.

Viktor Barie is a master student in the field of Business Management with Computer Science. The bachelor thesis is written in the context of the scientific specialization Controlling, where Gamification and Crowding Out are relevant aspects for analyzing human behavior and decisions.

References

Deci, E. L. (1971). Effects of Externally Mediated Rewards on Intrinsic Motivation. Journal of Personality and Social Psychology, 18 (1971), i. 1, 105-115.

Deci, E. L., Koestner, R., & Ryan, R. M. (1999). A Meta-Analytic Review of Experiments Examining the Effects of Extrinsic Rewards on Intrinsic Motivation. Psychological Bulletin, 125 (1999), i. 6, 627-668.

Deterding, S. (2011). A Quick Buck by Copy and Paste. Retrieved July 24, 2015, from http://gamification-research.org/2011/09/a-quick-buck-by-copy-and-paste/

Deterding, S. (2014). Eudaimonic Design, Or: Six Invitations to Rethink Gamification. In Fuchs, M. et al. (Eds.), Rethinking Gamification (pp. 305-331), Lüneburg: Meson Press.

Deterding, S. et al. (2011a). From Game Design Elements to Gamefulness: Defining "Gamification". In Proceedings of the 15th International Academic MindTrek Conference: Envisioning Future Media Environments, (2011a), 9-15.

Deterding, S. et al. (2011b). Gamification: Using Game Design Elements in Non-Gaming Contexts. In: CHI '11 Extended Abstracts on Human Factors in Computing Systems, (2011b), 2425-2428.

Frey, B. S., & Jegen, R. (2000). Motivation Crowding Theory: A Survey of Empirical Evidence. In CESifo Working Paper Series, (2000), Nr. 245.

Frey, B. S., & Jegen, R. (2001a). Motivational Interactions: Effects on Behaviour. Annales d'Économie et de Statistique, (2001a), i. 63/64, 131-153.

Frey, B. S., & Jegen, R. (2001b). Motivation Crowding Theory. Journal of Economic Surveys, 15 (2001b), i. 5, 589-611.

Grant, S., & Betts, B. (2013). Encouraging User Behaviour with Achievements: An Empirical Study. 10th IEEE Working Conference on Mining Software Repositories (MSR), (2013), 65-68.

Hamari, J., Koivisto, J., & Sarsa, H. (2014). Does Gamification Work? – A Literature Review of Empirical Studies on Gamification. 47th Hawaii International Conference on System Science, (2014), 3025-3034.

Heeks, R. (2010). Understanding "Gold Farming" and Real-Money Trading as the Intersection of Real and Virtual Economies. Virtual Economies, Virtual Goods and Service Delivery in Virtual Worlds, 2 (2010), i. 4, 3-27.

Homburg, C. (2014). Marketingmanagement, 5. edition, Wiesbaden, Deutschland: Gabler Verlag.

Huotari, K., & Hamari, J. (2011). "Gamification" from the perspective of service marketing. CHI '11 Workshop Gamification. Retrieved July 24, 2015, from

http://gamification-research.org/wp-content/uploads/2011/04/14-Huotari.pdf

Huhh, J.-S. (2006). Effects on Real-Money Trading on MMOG Demand: A Network Externality Based Explanation. Retrieved July 24, 2015, from

http://ssrn.com/abstract=943368

Ryan, R. M., & Deci, E. K. (2001). Intrinsic and Extrinsic Motivations: Classic Definitions and New Directions. Contemporary Educational Psychology, 25 (2000), i. 1, 54-67.

Stack exchange inc. (2015). Welcome to Stack Overflow. Retrieved July 24, 2015, from

http://stackoverflow.com/tour

Taylor, T. L. (2012). Raising the Stakes. London, UK: The MIT Press.

Werbach, K., & Hunter, D. (2012). For The Win – How GAME THINKING Can Revolutionize your Business. Philadelphia, USA: Wharton Digital Press

Zichermann, G., & Cunningham, C. (2011). Gamification by Design. Sebastopol, CA: O'Reilly & Associates.

ONLINPCS:
From Olympics to Eletrônics

By Isaque Renovato de Araujo, Fernando Porfírio Soares de Oliveira

The Olympics as well as any other event or sport undergo changes from time to time, updating and modernizing motivated by the social context which it belongs. Therefore, with the current dynamics of information mainly due to the internet dynamics changed with the spread of new sports come up growing a sport that can pervade the design of traditional sport only as something to be done by people physically athletic, which it is the eSport or electronic sports.

The growth of the practitioners of this new form of electronic sports performance is still relatively new and because of the exponential pressure for them to be officially recognized as a sport in some countries in the world, to the point that among the various existing eSports, including, League of Legends (LoL), which due its popularity represented by the significant amount of practitioners, spectators and influence within the eSports. The point that it can discuss its worldwide acceptance as an Olympic sport and brings up the discussion that to be accepted as such, may have its definitive inclusion in the Olympics.

In the literature, Machado (2012), Rubio (2011) Turini (2002), exposed as were the Olympics in ancient Greece and how they have changed in regards to his philosophy and how its purpose, however, in the current context with connectivity and technological evolution begins to be research on electronic sports that because they have not linked these athletes with Olympian features suffer prejudice and are not yet considered as athletes, is the fact that most of the athlete's design be tied to a specific physical size or the lack of full acceptance of the electronic sports as sports.

Such a change of the sports paradigm for this new reality comes into existence, in which the eSports emerges as a new sport, which may be recognized as Olympic in the present context does not appear to be something distant of reality and values of the Olympic world.

For the survey, data was collected about how the Olympics and their situational changes, and will analyze the game League of Legends glimpsing its impact from championships, players and eSports market as a whole.

Then the above is the issue of research, will be insusceptible eSports be compatible as Olympic sport and are in line with their philosophy?

Olympics and eSports: An Analysis Overview

In its original conception the Olympics in Greece were initially conceived as a religious festival in honor of Zeus and was practiced in the sanctuary of Olympia. It was considered as Olympic sports in that time, pedestrian races, horse races, pentathlon and fights sparring and pankration. According to Machado

(2012) the only ones eligible to join those was the male citizens considered free men, excluding, therefore, women, slaves and barbarians.

Historically we know that the Olympics were held until the year 392 AD when they were suspended by King Theodosius I, with the theme of Olympians Games as in ancient Greece taken over by Baron de Coubertin in 1892 on the 5th anniversary of the Union of French Societies of Sports athletic (Rubio 2011).

Soon after its reopening, the next step was the establishment of the International Olympic Committee (IOC) that in its foundation was conceived as an institution that would use an oligarchic model, that is, the members of the committee would be since its foundation nominated by oldest and so on. Such option by Coubertin was made in order to avoid internal conflicts due to democracy, and to guide the Committee's actions was formulated the Olympic letter that has at its core three main purposes:

• Establish principles and values of Olympism;
• Serve as the IOC code;
• Set rights and obligations of the three main constituents of the Olympic Movement: the IOC, the International Federations and the National Olympic Committees and the Organizing Committee of each edition of the Games. (IOC 2015, p. 11).

The Olympic letter went through reformulations according to the passing time in the board meetings, and added new rules as global issues, and today in 2015 has 6 chapters and 61 subchapters. In these meetings the board also act on the letter of the translation to other languages, with the proviso that always prevail to any questions the translation that prevails is the French.

Coubertin has proposed the resumption of the Olympics in 1900 as the turn of the centennial, but the games were advanced for its reopening in 1896 in Athens in order to reference the Olympic Games in antiquity. (Rubio 2011).

> "It is important, however take into consideration that the way they were designed the Olympics of the modern era and their differing purposes of its original, Tavares (1999) says that this new way of presenting the Olympics served not only as a means of socializing and competition between participants, but as an educational medium, moral and social, in which one of the objectives arising from this event would be the social growth by society".

Therefore, social development is related as values and concepts that underlie the modern Olympic assumptions being understood as fair play. This concept is understood in the literature as the values to be followed, which are guiding for any athlete and therefore should be linked to everything that the Olympics represent. Turini (2002) in his article search a little deeper than would be the concept of fair play:

It is important to the understanding of fair play as an element that has its genesis in England and acquired spread through Olympism. Thus means fair play as one of Olympism values, considered the sport ethics of modern sport that is intended to guide the conduct competitive in sports. The general idea of fair play as the attitude of a good behavior is associated with the chivalrous behavior that had its genesis in England. Chivalry, an existing European social behavior in the nineteenth century, meant the noble, honorable and honest man (chivalric ethos), from the Western Christian values and human values related to the Renaissance. Hence, the strong influence of English social model in the formation of fair play. Coubertin transferred the principles of social behavior model as the ethical reference of sports practice at the universal level (p. 220).

The modern Olympics went still other changes, among them the number of sports modalities, where in ancient times there were 9 modalities, while in 2016 in Rio de Janeiro will be 39 modalities that make up this edition of the Olympics, the first ever to be held in a country of Latin america. These modalities are likely to change according to the IOC, which always intersperse between modalities and decide which sports can be considered Olympic, but sometimes some sports take decades to come to be quoted in competition such as the Golf that since 1904 is not selected and the Rugby since 1924.

eSports, the sport of the digital era

Electronic sports, or as they are better known eSports are currently increasingly in evidence because of their dynamic virtual integration network that enables access "to all" in real time, but its appearance is relatively old, dating 93 in the journal wired the game Netrek as "the first online sport" (Hiltscher, 2014) and Following Wagner (2006) eSports refer to the late '90s in which began officially to use the term for online Gamers Association (OGA), which in your Mat Bettingtn foundation compared eSports traditional sports, but although there the denomination sports the same are still considered only as games in various parts of the world, a fact that is wrongly had since according Galatti (2012) the game is set as a playful character of activity with standards established freely by the participants. The sport, in turn, has rules pre-established by the various institutions that govern each sport.

Currently there are more than 50 games that are considered eSports since they have pre-established rules and are controlled by regulatory institutions, among the various types of eSports one that can be considered the greatest style called MOBA (multiplayer online battle arena) in amount of practitioners is League of Legends that according to data from developer RIOT currently has 67 million accounts worldwide, also having a major style championships which in turn ensure the awards in large amounts (average of $2,000,000) losing only to another eSport of the same style (DOTA 2) in a matter of values prizes. As table 01 shows the 5 eSports championships and larger amounts of athletes each.

Major eSports titles		
eSports game	Athletes	Championships
Dota 2	1288	480
League of Legends	3546	1542
Starcraft 2	1393	3091
Counter-Strike	2530	562
Counter-Strike: Global Offensive	3093	938

Figure 1: Tournament landsacpe in eSports (adapted from http://www.esportsearnings.com/games)

The company also has partnerships with companies products for gamers and other segments such as Coca-Cola and as in other eSports encouraged the professionalization of its practitioners, with such a significant impact to the point to make in some countries like the United States and South Korea pro-players being considered athletes and eSports as sports. Such action as well as promoting the growth of practitioners also allows it to be possible that scholarships are offered at universities, giving an educational counterpart encouraging the study.

However, by the society there is still no complete agreement concerning the respect eSports as sports and its practitioners as athletes.

To this end, it is important to understand what can be defined as a sport and as an athlete to be able to then assess inquiries. Marques (p, 366, 2009) defines sport as follows:

> "It is normally sport setting as a sociocultural phenomenon that includes several human practices, guided by rules of its own and institutionalized action, directed to a competitive aspect, whether it is characterized by the contrast between subject and by comparing the individual's own accomplishments, which manifest through body activity. These practices can express themselves through direct confrontations between subjects, but always express the desire for fulfillment of the human being that embodies the need, among others, to thrill, be overcome, play, play and communicate".

Some authors as well take into account the physical effort and to be a sports activity should occur in formal conditions and organized state that there should be some complexity in the movements (Barbanti, 2006).

In view of the conditions to make a distinction between an athlete and a person who only practice in an amateur way eSports can also list the number of shares and reasoning that is spent during their practice in which a professional athlete can do to 300 actions per minute while an enthusiast is on average 50 shares. When seeking an athletic conceptualization there are not so many criteria to be defined, however, in Brazil, one can make the distinction between those who can be called professional athletes and non-professionals by Law No. 9.615 of 24 March 1998 establishing general rules on sport and other provisions in article 3 which reads as follows: Sole Paragraph - performance sports can be organized and practiced:

> I - a professional, characterized by the remuneration agreed in formal labor contract between the athlete and the organization of sports practice;
> II - non-professional manner, identified by freedom of practice and the lack of employment contract, which allowed the receipt of material incentives and sponsorship.

As in other sports, preparation and training of athletes are strictly followed, in which it is observed that there are times to study matches, tactics and some slacks cases are rare moments that can only be post championship applications because of its importance . generally having as concentration gaming houses that are homes that serve to host athletes, usually those who are sponsored and staff spend not only in the weeks leading championships, but longer periods aimed at performance and high performance in sport practiced.

By observing these requirements is noticeable the framework by the eSports and its participants respectively sport and athletes.

Viewing this fact another question comes up, that is about the recognition of the eSports effectively as sport and on the possible inclusion of these in future editions of the Olympics by the IOC.

The concept of Olympic sport includes some specific criteria that must be met so that they can be guided in the meetings of the IOC and be inserted in the games. Among general criteria is mentioned primarily concern at the scope and practitioners in the world where the sport should be practicing at least by men in

at least 75 countries and 4 continents and by women in at least 40 countries and 3 continents.
The remaining 39 criteria are divided into eight themes as follows: general, governance, history and tradition, universality, popularity, athletes, sports development and finance. They serve to assess the entry of the respective sports in the Olympics (IOC, 2012).

When comparing both information we can see that not only the criteria are satisfactory as it is also possible to state that the proposed article to infer that LoL can be classified as a sport and fits perfectly with Olympism criteria, since according to Olympic primer (p 3, 2010) Olympism can be defined as follows:

Olympism is a philosophy of life that advocates the formation of a pacifist conscience, democratic, humanitarian, cultural and ecological through sports.

The goal of Olympism is to place sport at the service of man, from the creation of a lifestyle based on the joy of physical exertion and respect among citizens, contributing to the development of the individual and strengthening understanding and unity among people.

The ideals of Olympism are: mass participation; education through sport; the promotion of collective spirit, cultural exchange and international understanding, and the pursuit of excellence.

Based on these ideals, the Olympic Movement arises, based on solidarity for the development of the world and equality in economic, social and cultural order. One of its main goals is to offer young people around the world the possibility of achieving high sports level, without any discrimination.

Within the Olympic Movement: the International Olympic Committee (IOC), National Olympic Committees, sports organizations, athletes and all who accept the Olympic Charter.

As light of such criteria, a comparison is necessary with information from official League of Legends data and the general criteria and the official ideals of Olympism guided by the IOC.

Olympic criteria and Olympism	League of Legends (LoL)
75 countries and 4 continents	Any country having internet, therefore also found on all continents
Players gender	Since the practice is online does not care gender, or any other feature except for the performance in game, such features are irrelevant.
It has defined rules	Yes, all competitions are regulated and monitored by the developer, as well as in its manifesto emphasizes how everyone must behave.
Mass participation	67 million players (RIOT Manifesto 2015)
Education through sport	League of Legends encourages logical thinking, strategic, stock speed. As well as in countries like the United States and South Korea scholarships are given to athletes.

Promoting collective spirit	The community is permeated by the fact of not being primarily need to be specifically in a place to enter competitions and interact with people around the globe
Cultural exchange and international understanding	Being online with no physical or geographical barriers allows interaction with people from various other places and cultures.
Pursuit of excellence	The manifesto RIOT encourages all players values growth, but he should not forget to be humble.

Figure 2: Comparative table with the general criteria of the Olympics and ideals of Olympism.

Based on these we can see that given historical sports developments and the growth of eSport the reinvention of the modern Olympics is something that might happen with its permanent acceptance, given that the world is rapidly changing and this change is also necessary to meet the global demands of those who enjoy the event.

Comparing the information exposed previously in the table realizes the universality with which LoL can include anyone who wishes to practice, but it does so without having made any distinction showing irrelevance of gender, nationality and social class.

Research Methodology

This study was conducted using qualitative research, in which Creswell (2010), cites as a means to explore and to understand the meaning that individuals or groups attach a social or human problem. Minayo (2001) complements saying it works with the universe of meanings, reasons, aspirations, beliefs, values and attitudes.

The article can be characterized as a case study since it according to Yin (2001) a case study is an empirical observation that investigates a contemporary phenomenon within its real-life context, especially when the boundaries between the phenomenon and the context does not they are clearly defined.

As technical collection and processing of data from documents and collected literature was made the analysis of the content Bardan (2006) defines this as being not only as an instrument, but a broad, comprehensive range that requires the researcher's time and dedication and to explore and delve into the subject there are new codes to be analyzed thus increasing the complexity of the whole.

In view of the objectives of this study that evaluated eSports more precisely League of Legends as a possible new Olympic sport were raised official data of RIOT with quantity practitioners, rules, along with IOC's data with criteria and Olympic philosophies and literature search in order to support the subject in focus and complete the research in question in the context that it was analyzed.

Final Considerations

It is possible that changes across the medium and growth by those interested in the eSports embodiment will be officially accepted worldwide as sport, for to do an analysis of what can be considered the sport they fall.

In Racing acceptance of League of Legends as Olympic sport is possible after analysis of the criteria, along with documentary analysis note that comply with the IOC advocates, however we can also understand that the lack of an international federation can come to delay this fact, along with the very agenda of the IOC, since it does not work in a democratic manner the interest of members is an imperative that such issues are raised.

For the preparation of the article there were limitations on access to data that is available on the internet with regard to RIOT, since its internal policy prevents specific data to be disclosed as much practitioners targeted by country, age and other related information. Such restrictions are given by their organizational form and transparency which may hinder its acceptance by the IOC. What hindered the foundation to fully examine the possibility of LoL accepted as Olympic. However the future with the creation of an eSports federation to better regulate and assist in the expansion, many of these data may be disclosed, giving transparency to the practitioners of the sport there are world-view that LoL is still a recent eSport improvements in its political will come along with other eSports.

As the theme is still something going on and new, are new questions to be made about the growth and acceptance of eSports and its practitioners, and the impact of sports virtual dynamic since its practice may seem strange to traditional practitioners other sports, but to observe their impact on society and its agreement with what is encouraged by the Olympic philosophy, we see that not varied from the goals of the olympics, but being able to be permanently included in its future editions.

Isaque Renovato de Araujo - isaquerenovato@gmail.com - Master's of business administration by Universidade Federal do Rio Grande do Norte and works as a data analyst and social analyst for IT companies

Fernando Porfirio Soares de Oliveira - Doctorate at Administration from Universidade Federal do Rio Grande do Norte (2014). Currently professor at Universidade Federal Rural do Semi-Árido.

References

Barbanti, V. O Que é Esporte? Revista Brasileira de Atividade Física e Saúde. Pelotas, v. 11, n. 1, 54-58, jan. 2006. Recuperado setembre 29, 2015, de: http://periodicos.ufpel.edu.br/ojs2/index.php/RBAFS/article/viewFile/833/840

Bardin, L. (2006). Análise de conteúdo. Lisboa: Edições 70.

Brasil Lei nº 9615, de 24 de março de 1998. Legislação Desportiva. Sítio eletrônico internet - planalto.gov.br

Carta olímpica (olympic charter). Recuperado Oktober 7, 2015, de: http://www.olympic.org/Documents/olympic_charter_en.pdf

Cartilha Olímpica. Recuperado Oktober 7, 2015, de: http://www.cbca.org.br/arquivos/ckfinder/files/cartilha_olimpismo.pdf

Creswell, J. W. Projeto de pesquisa: métodos qualitativo, quantitativo e misto. 3.ed. Porto Alegre: Artmed/Bookman, 2010.

Evaluation criteria for sports and disciplines. Recuperado Setembre 29, 2015, de: http://www.olympic.org/Documents/Commissions_PDFfiles/Programme_commission/2012-06-12-IOC-evaluation-criteria-for-sports-and-disciplines.docx.pdf

Galatti, L. R. Qual a diferença entre jogo e esporte. Revista Nova Escola. Recuperado Oktober 16, 2015, de: http://revistaescola.abril.com.br/fundamental-1/qual-diferenca-jogo-esporte-656036.shtml.

Hiltscher, J. A Short Story of eSports. eSports yearbook 2013/2014. Recuperado Dezembro 1, 2015, de: http://www.esportsyearbook.com/eyb1314.pdf

Lista de eSports mais praticados. Recuperado Setembro 29, 2015, de: http://www.esportsearnings.com/games/

Machado, R. P. T., Valor Cultural E Ético Do "Espetáculo Esportivo" Na Grécia Antiga, PODIUM: Sport, Leisure and Tourism Review, São Paulo, v. 1, n. 1, p. 47-65, jan./jun. 2012

Manifesto RIOT games. Recuperado Setembro 29, 2015, de: http://www.riotgames.com/pt-br/o-manifesto-riot

Marques, R.F.R. Esporte olímpico e paraolímpico: coincidências, divergências e especificidades numa perspectiva contemporânea. Revista Brasileira de Educação Física e Esporte, São Paulo, v.23, n.4, 2009.

Rubio, Katia, A dinâmica do Esporte olímpico do século XIX ao XXI, Rev. bras. Educ. Fís. Esporte, São Paulo, v.25, 83-90, 2011

Rotina de treino de mushi. Recuperado Oktober 7, 2015, de: https://www.facebook.com/mushichai/

Turini, M., & Dacosta, L., A prática do Fair Play A prática do Fair Play no contexto da no contexto da culturalidade, Coletânea de textos em estudos olímpicos, v. 01, Rio de Janeiro: Editora Gama Filho, 2002

Wagner, M. G., On the Scientific Relevance of eSports. Recuperado Setembro 29, 2015, de: http://ww1.ucmss.com/books/LFS/CSREA2006/ICM4205.pdf.

Yin, R.K. Estudo de caso: planejamento e métodos. 2. ed. Porto Alegre: Bookman, 2001.

eSports in Korea: A Study on League of Legends Team Performances on the Share Price of Owning Corporations

By Filbert Goetomo

In Korea many large corporations sponsor eSports teams to compete in various different video games under their brand. As a firm's share price is often a function of people's perception of a firm, it is hypothesized that positive events such as beginning a sponsorship or a team's success during a tournament or campaign season will increase the value of a firm's shares whilst a loss will negatively impact them. Mackinlay (1997) demonstrates an event study by 'using financial market data' to 'measure the impact of a specific event on the value of a firm.' Given the nature of the market place, the market should quickly adjust to compensate for the effects of events, adjustments that will be immediately reflected in the firm's share prices. As such, the economic impact of an event can be measured by observing the changes in security prices (Mackinlay, 1997).

The History of eSports and the rise of League of Legends

In the words of Jack Ma, 'We're not investing in football, we're investing in entertainment...Alibaba's future strategies are health and entertainment'. And he is not the only one with that mind set. As the 21st century continues to mature, firms are seeing the value in new and somewhat untraditional industries that have grown in leaps and bounds in recent years. One of these industries is that of eSports.

Electronic sports, otherwise known as eSports is a form of mental sports where participants contend with each other in various different video games. Although to most this may seem like an unheard of branch of sports, competitive gaming has existed for much longer than one would expect. In 1980 Atari hosted the first video game tournament featuring one of the most iconic retro games in existence, Space Invaders (Edwards, 2013). Space Invaders is a simple game where the player controls a side scrolling spaceship strafing the earth' s atmosphere at the base of the screen. The objective of the game is to shoot down rows of aliens as they descend towards Earth. The tournament featured 4 regional competitors, including the representative of Chicago who was already being sponsored. The contestants were flown out to New York City to compete in the nationals of Space invaders. The tournament was won by Rebecca Heineman who took home a stand-up arcade cabinet. Heineman would go on to work on titles such as Bard's Tale and Dragon Wars while the competitive video game industry would also continue to grow and feature competitions of increasing scale and prestige. 1997 featured what is considered by many to the first 'real' video game tournament with Dennis 'Thresh' Fong winning a Ferrari 328 GTS for his championship winning performance on the First Person Shooter (FPS) Quake'.

Launched in 2009, by Riot Games, League of Legends is a free to play spin off of the classic Multiplayer Online Battle Arena (MOBA) genre. Being the first and only title released by the firm, Riot Games was quick in taking advantage of the genre's inherently competitive and strategic gameplay and creating multiple championships and tournaments, attracting hundreds of thousands of players to their rapidly growing fan base. The championships became known as the League Championship Series (LCS). As Marc Merill, Co-founder and President of Riot Games said, "We lose a lot of money on eSports. It's not something, currently, that we do to drive return or profitability…if we bring value to our players, they'll reward us with engagement" (Tran, 2012). Riot generates a variety of different content outside the game itself, such as the weekly Championship matches, analysis and eSports articles.

The Game

The basics of a MOBA is incredibly simple. The game features two teams of 5 players, each of whom controls a single champion. Waves of allied computer controlled minions are spawned down three lanes from each team's home base in a relentless attempt to push the other team back and destroy the opposing nexus. The role of the player is to aid these minions in their push whether this is by destroying opposing champions, minions or turrets. Of course the game grows exponentially more complex when there are over 120 different champions to choose from. Each have their own unique mechanics and abilities that interact differently with various other champions and as such many hours of practice are required to master each Champion and all of its unique facets.

Furthermore, outside of the three lanes, other objectives are scattered throughout the arena in zones known as 'the jungle'. Example include a Dragon that give bonus stats to your team, the blue sentinel which grants a single player faster mana regeneration and cool down reduction (a shorter minimum delay between spell casts) and the Baron grants your team and minions bonus stats as well as a large amount of gold to spend on items. As such, controlling these objectives, synergising as a team and even selecting the best champions to execute your strategy turns an otherwise simple affair into an extremely strategically in-depth contest of skill and wits.

The standard 'meta game' or, essentially the standard strategic setup of the 5 members of a team include one 'top laner' and one 'mid laner', each of whom will primarily defend the top and mid lane respectively. The bottom lane is held by two players, the 'AD (Attack damage) Carry' and his partner the 'Support'. These players are supplemented by the final member of their roster, the 'Jungler' whom roams unseen through the jungle applying pressure to the enemy.

Not only is the game fun and entertaining for individuals to play but watching professional's play the game at the highest level is also incredibly rewarding as not only does it offer an insight into how one can improve oneself but professionals are also capable of working seamlessly together as a team or perform highly technical in game manoeuvres that the average individual could only ever dream of achieving.

Being free to play, Riot's profits come from players purchasing an in game premium currency known as 'Riot Points' to unlock what is, for the most part, purely aesthetic content for their avatars. To maintain a level playing field, premium currency is unable to purchase goods that will give a player a competitive edge over another. The low barriers to entry of a free to play game with a low skill floor, albeit, a high skill ceiling has made the game exceedingly accessible to the public.

The Competitive format and Korea

Before the formation of the LCS, throughout the year, many different organisations such as the eSports League (ESL) or Intel would organise tournaments throughout the year where teams could earn circuit points.

These points work as an impromptu scoring system as without the existence of a formal league format, circuit points allowed Riot to objectively identify the best teams from around the world. At the conclusion of a season, Riot Games would invite the best teams to participate in the World Finals.

However, in 2012, Riot games launched fully professional gaming leagues around the world branding it the League Championship Series (LCS). Similar to English Football's Barclay's Premier League, teams will go head to head twice in a round robin format to claim the top position before being entered into the regional finals where the top teams are then invited to the World Championships. Similar to the UEFA Champions League of European football, the top ranked teams from each region will contend with each other for the crown of the best team in the world.

Korea was one of the early adopters of the eSports trend and in the year 2000, became one of the first nations to officially licence pro gamers, create the Korean e-Sport Association (KESPA) as well as expand the Ministry of Culture, Sports and Tourism to encompass the growing industry of Korean eSports. Before long, televised eSports became increasingly common place with OnGameNet and MBCGame televising regular tournaments of then popular games such as StarCraft: Broodwar and Warcraft III: The Frozen Throne on 24-hour cable TV game channels. In March of 2012, the first iteration of Korea's premier League of Legends Season began under the name 'OLYMPUS Champions Winter 2012-2013 where it is now known as the OnGameNet organised 'LoL Champions Korea' (LCK).

In Korea, eSports has, for a long time, been more than gaming. It has evolved into a way of life similar to Basketball in the United States or Football in South America. PC Bangs, or internet cafes are a staple throughout the nation as the South Korean youth immerse themselves in video games. To put it simply, in 1999, eSports debuted on South Korean television whilst over 15 years later, this is still a novel concept in the west. Thus, it comes as no surprise that Korean culture has evolved around eSports to the extent that Korean teams are owned and sponsored by Large Korean organizations, operating essentially as a form of marketing for these companies.

At the end of the Season 4 World Championship, the West and China poured excessive amounts of money into recruiting Korean players, individuals who were viewed to be much more talented and having a better understanding of the game. As such, a large number of Korean players departed their home country, motivated by foreign money, creating what is known as the Great Korean Exodus. Amongst the departing players was the entirety of the Season 4 winning roster as well as Season 3 world Champion 'Piglet'. The large talent drain on Korea left many wondering if the age of Korean supremacy was at an end. Korea answered by crushing the Season 5 competition and setting up an all Korean grand final where SKT T1 triumphed 3-1 over the ROX tigers.

One of the largest reasons for Korea's complete dominance over the scene is their advanced infrastructure. Whilst in the West, organizations are only beginning to embrace the benefits of gaming houses, coaches and creating the best possible environment for their players, over in Korea, a well-oiled machine continues to excel in what it has always exceled at, creating championship winning teams (Lockarus, 2015).

The Korean competitive league distinguishes itself from the other regions by favouring a best of three format to determine the winner of a set. In a season long round robin, each team will play two best of three sets against every other team in the league. At the end of a season the top 5 teams are entered into the playoffs, a best of five gauntlet styled tournament where the fifth seed takes on the fourth, the winner will take on the third and so on and so forth. The winner of the playoffs are crowned the season champions and earn a spot at either the World Finals or the Mid-Season Invitational, depending on if it is the Summer or Spring Season respectively.

Conversely, the bottom 2 teams of the regular season, the ninth and tenth placed teams, enter relegations and must play for their right to remain in the top flight by defeating the top two teams from the Korean 'Challenger series'. The challenger series being a league for aspiring amateur teams, similar to that of British football's 'Championship' division. Relegations is a chance of for these teams to earn the right to play in the LCK.

In the League of Legends scene, Azubu Frost was arguably the first highly successful Korean team, qualifying for the grand finals of the Season 2 World Championships where they fell 3-1 to the Taipei Assassins, a match that boasted over 1.1 million concurrent viewers. Until that period of time, that was the most watched eSports event of all time (Breslau, 2012).

In 2013, Korea returned with a vengeance when SK Telecom T1 defeated the Chinese first seed Royal Club 3-0 in the Grand finals to claim the crown of World Champions. This feat was accomplished with a peak viewership of over 8.5 million concurrent individuals (McCormick, 2013). To put this into perspective, more people watched the 2013 grand final than the 2013 NBA finals or the 2013 World Series (Schwartz, 2014).

Korea successfully defending their title in 2014 with Samsung White's victory and again in 2015 when SK Telecom T1 reclaimed their title in front of an ever growing number of fans. SK T crowned themselves two time champions in front of 334 million unique daily impressions, essentially the number of unique viewers who tuned in every day over the course of the 5 week tournament (Figueira, 2015).

One of the largest differing factors between Western eSports and Korean eSports is that teams in the West are owned by exclusively gaming firms whilst Korean eSports teams are generally backed by a major sponsor the team represents. This is usually a large corporation with business interests outside of professional gaming, for example, Korean Air, in the aviation industry. As such, this study is made possible by focussing on Korean teams owned by publicly traded corporations. This thesis will attempt to measure how the team's welfare, be it success or failure, will have a statistically significat effect on the firm's share prices.

Today, the LCK features a ten team league consisting of the Afreeca Freecs, CJ Entus, Jin Air Green Wings, Kongdoo Mosnter, Kt Rolster, Longzhu, Rox Tigers, Samsung, SBENU Sonicboom and SK Telecom T1. These teams compete 4 days a week in the regular season at the Yongsan E-Sports Stadium in Seoul, South Korea, the historic eSports arena home to Korean eSports for over a decade.

The Five Firms

Five companies were identified to be publicly traded and to have consistently sponsored teams through the many seasons of the LCK. These traits are important as they allow access to historical data of publicly traded stocks and shares. These firms are as follows: the CJ Corporation, Korean Air, Samsung, SK Telecom, and the Kt Corporation.

SK telecom is a subsidiary of one of the largest conglomerates in South Korea. Founded on the 8th of

April 1953 by the late Chey John-hyun, they changed their name in 1997 from the SunKyoung Group to the SK group. SK telecom is the largest wireless mobile phone service provider in South Korea. Created in 1984, as the Korea Mobile Telecommunications Services Corp., SK telecom grew to become the local market leader with a 50.5% share as of 2008 (Sun-Young, 2008). Dong-Hyun Jang was appointed CEO and president of this subsidiary in March of 2015 joining Dae-Sik Cho who have been in command since March 2013. The 2014 annual report indicated an 'annual revenue of KRW 17,163.8 billion, an operating profit of KRW 1,825.1 billion and net profit of KRW 1,799.3 billion' (SK Telecom Co., Ltd. Annual Report, 2014) Korea's most successful team, SK Telecom entered the scene by purchasing the roster of Eat Sleep Game to form SKT T1 S before later forming their sister team, SKT T1 K. Following the restructuring banning the use of sister teams, led by their talismanic captain Lee "Faker" Sang-Hyeok, SKT reformed into the current reigning two time World Champions, SKT T1.

The CJ Corporation was founded by Lee Byung – Chui as 'Cheil Jedang' in August of 1953 as a sugar and flour manufacturer and a part of the Samsung Group. Breaking away in 1996 and changing its name to the CJ Co., Ltd in 2002, the CJ Corporation is currently under the stewardship of Gyeong Sik Son, their CEO as well as chairmen Lee Jay-Hyun and Sohn Kyung-Shik (So-Hyun, 2013). Now evolving to produce in the film as well as Television broadcasting industries, CJ have grown into much more than a simple flour mill. CJ finished 2014 with sales of KRW 11,701,797 million, an operating profit of KRW 579,930 million and a gross income of KRW 2,443,371,595 million (CJ Financial Info, 2015). On the 24th of May 2012, CJ became one of the first sponsors to acquire a League of Legends team, sponsoring both CJ Entus Blaze and CJ Entus Frost. Despite having fielded some of League of Legend's finest players such as MakNooN, Ganked By Mom and CloudTemplar, CJ has never reached the dizzying heights of their colleagues.

The KT Corporation was founded as Korea Telecom in the winter of 1981 as a public utility. The company was privatized after 20 years in May 2001 and changed its name to KT although still remaining a telecom firm. The current CEO Chang-Gyu Hwang was appointed in 2014. Being South Korea's first telephone company, KT controls 90% of the country's fixed-line subscribers and 45% of high speed internet users (News World, 2006). KT's financial report as of December 31 2015 showed profits of KRW 631,288 million, operating revenue of KRW 22,281,221 and an operating profit of KRW 1,292,944 million. The KT Corporation sponsors a multi-gaming organization known as KT Rolster who entered the League of Legends scene with sister team Kt Rolster A and Kt Rolster B. Renaming to the Arrows and Bullets respectively, before restructuring to be known simply as KT Rolster.

Samsung is a multinational conglomerate founded by Lee Byung-chull 78 years ago in 1938 by Lee Byung-Chui as a trading company. Over the years, the firm expanded into diversifying fields such as food processing, insurance and of course, the electronics industry. Samsung is one of the largest firms in South Korea, making up 17% of South Korea's GDP in 2013 (Daniel, 2013). Samsung has been led by Chairman Lee Kun-hee since his reappointment in 2010. In 2015, Samsung boasted a gross profit of KRW 77,171,364 million, profits of KRW 19,060,144 million and revenues of KRW 200,653,482 million (Samsung Electronics Co., 2016). On the 7th of September 2013, Samsung entered the scene by acquiring and rebranding these the rosters of MVP Blue and MVP White into the sister teams Samsung White and Samsung Blue. The Samsung organization had their most successful year in 2014 with both teams qualifying for the world finals with Samsung White claiming the title after defeating Blue in the Semi-finals. Following the restructuring, Samsung is represented by Samsung Galaxy.

A low cost airline that begun operations in 2008, Jin Air, led by CEO Won Ma is a subsidiary of Korean Air. As Jin Air does not have publicly traded stocks, the study will instead incorporate Korean Air share prices to use as an approximate for Jin Air. In 1962, the South Korean Government founded Korean Air Lines as a rebranding of the Nationalized Korean National Airlines. Korean Air was privatized in 1969, becoming a part of the Hanjin Transport Group. Today, Korean Air is under the leadership of CEO Cho Yang Ho. Korean Air ended 2014 with a gross profit of KRW 1520204 million, an operating income of KRW 395,047 and sales of KRW 11,909,748 million (KoreanAir, 2015). On the 10th of September 2013, Jin Air obtained the rosters of Eat Sleep Game and Hood Good Day to form the Jin Air Green Wings Stealth and the Jin Air Green Wings Falcons. Despite their long presence in the league, the Green Wings have rarely challenged for the top position. However, as of late, this is likely to change.

The eSports market

In 2015, the eSports market was estimated to be approximately $612 Million in annual revenues with Asia, primarily China and Korea, dominating the industry with a controlling 61% share (Dreunen, 2015). This is a continually growing industry as annual viewership continues to rise rapidly. While 2012 featured approximately 58 million viewers and 2013, 74 million viewers, 2014 boasted 89 million viewers globally (Casselman,2015).

The League of Legends World Championships 2015 boasted a prize pool of over $2 million and while one may expect prize money to be a large sum of these earnings, as over half of which were claimed by the champions, to firms sponsoring their eSports teams, the prize money only represents a small portion of their earnings. In addition to the sale of merchandise, a large portion of profits are made from advertising and streaming. League of Legends garnered 20 Million viewers in their last World Championships and OnGamenet made $203 million last year from adverts played during streams and subscription fees alone. A stream is the modern day equivalent of cable television. A company may choose to 'stream', that is to say, essentially broadcast, live events directly to computers all over the world. Viewing is generally free of charge but viewers may have the option to enjoy the stream at a higher quality for a small subscription fee. Furthermore, streams are not limited to large gaming events. Rather, anyone can stream a game on platforms such as Azubu or Twitch Tv. Firms and individuals make a profit from the subscriptions to their 'channel' or the optional donations individuals may make to freely support their favourite entertainers, otherwise known as 'streamers'.

Last year, corporate sponsorship in North America totalled $111 million even including basketball legend Rick Fox purchasing his own team to compete in the Spring Split of the North American LCS. As such, due to massive the massive amounts of exposure the game receives, it quickly rose to prominence rapidly growing an enormous player base to become the most played PC game in 2015 (Statista, 2015).

In Korea, eSports suffered a setback between 2008 and 2012 with crises such as the decrease in interest of the then popular StarCraft Broodwar and the lack of interest in its successor, StarCraft 2. As such, the industry suffered greatly with broadcasters MBC Game discontinued in 2012 and OnGameNet only managing to survive by having a large portion of their eSports broadcasts removed from television broadcasts. Although Korea has yet to regain its title as the largest eSports economy in the world, they continue to recover at an incredible pace.

Prior Studies

One of the first event studies linking the performance of a sports team to fluctuations in the market was done by Brown and Hartzell (2001). The publicly traded Boston Celtics Limited Partnership allowed the results of the Celtic's basketball games to be correlated to the partnership's share returns, trading volume and volatility. The study also incorporated key event points such as the construction of the Boston Garden and the installation of Rick Pitino as head coach.

It was discovered that investors, to a degree, utilize match results as a function of their trading habits. Furthermore, it was observed that, excluding play-off related income and expenses, every extra win in a year led to an increase in net revenue of $0.06 per share the following year. One of the most significant results was the appointment of Rick Pitino as trading 'volume soars to about 70 times its daily average, and over the month of the even (approximately) the unit price rises $2, or 8.2%.' As such, these results show that for firms tied to sports, not only do on-field results matter but so do events related to the welfare of the team.

The findings of Coates and Humphreys (2008) reinforced these findings. By examining the effects of on-field success by Japanese baseball teams in the Nippon Professional baseball league and the fluctuations of the share prices of owning corporations, data showed that the idea that wins and losses have an effect on the owning corporation's share price returns, with losses posing a larger effect than wins (Coates & Humphreys, 2008).

Edmans, Garcia and Norli (2007) explored the relationship between stock market reactions and sudden changes in investor mood. A large sample of sports were selected, such as football, rugby and basketball as well as across regions such as North America, Europe and the Asia/Pacific region. Edmans et al. discovered was that there was, in fact, a significant market decline after game losses. For example, elimination from the World Cup will cause an abnormal stock return of -49 basis points. As well as this, across the entire sample size, sponsoring firms all attained abnormal returns of at least +0.36% on the date of the sponsorship announcement. Furthermore, the impact of a loss is more apparent in small stocks with more local investors as well as in in important games such as the grand finals. It was also noted that that size of the abnormal return was inversely proportional to the size of the firm, this may be due to the fact that the effect of a sponsorship on a smaller firm is much more visible as there is potentially less external 'noise' influencing the data as well as a higher incremental awareness increase for smaller firms.

Kim's thesis in 2013 is an event study that builds on this past research as a closer look was taken into Chinese and Korean football teams and how both positive and negative events pertaining to these teams affect the share prices of the owner corporations (Kim, 2014). Kim's thesis contributes to the growing literature that ownership of a football club possesses a degree of economic returns on investment which is reflected in the share price returns of owning corporations resulting in a quantifiable win-win scenarios for both the club and for corporation. For example it was shows that there was a 'positive and significant effect of the acquisition of Guangzhou Evergrande FC by Evergrande Group on March 1, 2010'. Kim also highlighted the significance of player transfers in share price returns, citing examples such as the Ianis Zicu transfer to the Pohang Steelers FC on the 4th of January 2012 and the Darko Matic transfer to Beijing Guoan FC on the 4th of February 2009.

One specific type of event that this thesis will observe is the effects of a firm's announcement of sponsoring a new team. Reiser, Breur and Wicker (2012) show the effect of sponsorship announcements on the firm's value. Taking data from 1999 to 2010, an event study analyzed the data for a variety of different sports across various different regions. Results showed that sponsorship announcements have a positive effect on the sponsor's share price returns. However, the level of impact is not consistent throughout sport or region with abnormal returns being significantly higher for sponsorship deals with a national reach.

In addition to this, the benefits of sponsorships are twofold. Kamakura (1995) analyzed the effects of announcements of celebrity endorsement contracts, finding results that on average indicate a positive effect on stock returns, implying that celebrity endorsements are a worthwhile investment in advertising. With eSports being one of the pillars of Korean culture, Korean's have placed their eSports athletes in the same social standing as any athlete or movie celebrity would be in the West. As such, a firm has the double incentive to invest into a team as investors are not only rewarded with a positive increase in share price returns but also from the celebrity endorsements of these athletes (Young, 2015).

As the literature has shown, the effect of sponsorship deals have a quantifiable impact on the share prices of sponsoring companies, making itself apparent in the form of abnormal returns. Furthermore, the performance of an on field sports team have also been shown to directly correlate to the share price return of a sponsoring firm. As such, the question must be asked, will the same apply to a smaller yet, rapidly growing, industry such as eSports?

Methodology

The efficient market hypothesis states that firms will have abnormal returns, that is to say, when events concerning the company and thus, their sponsored teams are both unforeseen and relevant to future performances, returns will be non-zero. Alternatively, the null hypothesis implies 0 correlation between a team's performance and the company's share prices meaning an event will not cause a statistically significant shift in a company's share price. Events such as the transfer of players, both the acquisition of new talent and the departure of a member of the roster have also been incorporated as these factors enhance the team's value as well as impact the teams expected future performances.

The efficient market hypothesis also assumes that all individuals have an equal amount of access to information resulting in stocks being perfectly priced based on all previous knowledge. As such, market efficiency will reflect the impact of eSports related events.

Five firms that have been consistent in sponsoring a League of Legends team (or in some cases, two teams) over an extended period of time. These firms are the CJ Corporation, Korean Air, Samsung, SK Telecom and The KT cooperation. For these firms events were identified that were likely to impact shares of the firm. These events will include victories and defeats in important matches, such as a final, winning a trophy and beginning a sponsorship contract. The event window (the minimum number of observations before and after the event date) and estimation window (the minimum number of observations before the event window) chosen are ±1 days and 15 and 30 days respectively.

As the duration of a tournament rarely exceeds a month, an estimation window of between 15 and 30 days were selected so as to attempt to capture the effect of the tournament's progression on investor's expectations in the days leading up the grand finals. As for the event window, although short horizon event windows are, relative to long horizon event windows, more powerful, this is only the case if abnormal returns are generated around the date of the event. Unfortunately in some cases, the effects of an event may not be fully captured within a short window. Nevertheless, a long horizon estimation window may be too loosely defined resulting in data that captures an excess of external noise, interfering and confounding the data. As such, for the case of eSports, a short event window was preferred. A difference of 1 day on either side of the event was selected as the share prices were expected to quickly adjust to the events with no lingering effects or aftershocks after the main event.

As event studies observe abnormal returns due to the significance of prominent events, the normal performance of a specific parent company will be calculated using a market model designed by Eugene Fama in 1969. Assuming a linear relationship between the daily returns of the firm and the daily returns of the relevant value-weighted market index.

$$Rft = \alpha f + \beta fRmkt + eft.$$

Where Rft is the daily return of the firm at time t, αf is the intercept, and βf is the coefficient of Rmkt which is the daily return of the value-weighted market index and eft is the error for firm f.

Brown and Warner (1980) discovered that 'beyond a simple, one factor market model, there is no evidence that more complicated methodologies convey any benefit. In fact, we have presented evidence that more complicated methodologies can actually make the researcher worse off".

This model has the daily return of the firm as the dependent variable and the daily return of the value-weighted market index as the independent variable. The benchmark normal return is the return around the event window that would have followed in the absence of any shift.

Abnormal returns are calculated by subtracting the estimated normal returns from the actual returns of the event date.

$$ARft = 1\frac{\sum ARft}{\delta ARft} - \hat{\beta}f\ Rmkt.$$

Cumulative abnormal returns were then calculated by adding all the abnormal returns for the firm. If the null hypothesis holds in which the event has no significant impact on share price, the abnormal return should be normally determined with a 0 conditional mean and variance.

The significance of the abnormal returns was calculated by means of a t-test. This was obtained through the division of the cumulative abnormal return by the standard deviation of abnormal returns. The statistical significance will be determined at the 90%, 95%, and at the 99% level which corresponds to absolute statistical values of 1.64, 1.96, and 2.58.

Data

Selected dates

The dates selected for the study correlates to events that were hypothesized to potentially be statistically significant and thus impact the average daily returns of the firm. Selected dates include the conclusion of an important championship, the transfer of a talented player, sponsorship deals and impactful rulings made my Riot Games or Kespa. To maintain precision and confounding effects on the data, dates that had overlapping event windows were omitted.

The daily returns of the CJ Corporation, Korean Air, SK Telecom Co Ltd, Samsung Electronics Co Ltd, the Kt Corporation and the Korea Stock Exchange Kospi Index were obtained from the Bloomberg database. As the Jin Air Green Wings were sponsored by Jin Air, a subsidiary of Korean air the share prices of Korean air was as an approximate of Jin Air share prices as Jin Air are not publicly traded. Days in which no trading took place were omitted from the data set so as to ensure that the estimation windows do not include any zero observations.

Player Transfers

Another important aspect of the game is the purchase and sale of players to and from an organization. Some of the events selected below attempt to capture these transfers by marking the announcement of a departure or arrival of a player. Whilst there is currently very limited way in which to quantifiably judge a player's performance, these players were selected due to the high regard in which they are held by other professionals, the community and those knowledgeable in the scene.

Throughout the existence of the formal professional League of Legends circuit, the ruling that distinguished itself in having shaken up the gaming world. On the 28th of October 2014 and largely impacted Korea in that a single organization is now limited to being able to field only a single team (Deesing, 2014).

Rulings

Throughout the existence of a formal professional League of Legends circuit, the ruling that distinguish itself in having shaken up the gaming world. On the 28th of October 2014 and largely impacted Korea in that a single organization is now limited to being able to field only a single team (Deesing, 2014).

For some Korean organizations, this meant merging their two sister teams into a main team with substitutes. For most Korean organizations, such as the then dominant Samsung who sent a quarter finalist and the eventual World Champion into the 2014 World Finals, this meant keeping as many of their best players as possible and getting as much as possible on the sales of their departing World finalists (Deesing, 2014). For the majority of these players, their future lay outside Korea in wealthier regions such as North America and China. These regions could afford a higher salary for these players, an important consideration given that for the average professional gamer, careers are short with very little to look forwards to after retirement. Furthermore, Korean talent is unquestionably higher than that of any other region, winning 3 of the last 5 World Championships and even having an all Korean final in the last finals. This ruling became known as the Korean exodus with Korea losing the majority of its talent abroad.

Concerning the dates selected for the rule change, each team will have a second date associated with this rule change. The date where they announce their single consolidated roster. Unfortunately, for some teams, this date was unavailable as changes were slowly made to the roster over the course of one or two months.

Tournament placings

A larger emphasis was placed on summer tournaments as spring and winter competitions held little to no significance whilst summer tournaments were often directly correlated to qualifications to the World Championships. The main criteria for tournaments selected was the prestige of the tournament, or its significance, for example, the Regional Finals, of which the victor will receive a seed and therefore a place in the World Finals. The event date used for the results was the final day of the tournament in which the observed team competed in. That is to say, the point in the competition where the team was either eliminated, or crowned the victor.

Results

Findings concerning the share price reactions of the CJ Corporation are divided into two categories, the significance of events with an estimation window of 15 days and an estimation window of 30 days. In both cases, the event window remained constant at one day on either side of the event.

With a 15 day Event Window, a number of events concerning the CJ corporations were statistically significant. Notably, the entrance of the company onto the Esports s scene with the creation of their own roster on the 24th of May 2012 possesses a statistical significance at the 99%, as well as the acquisition of both Azubu rosters creating the sister teams CJ Entus Frost and CJ Entus Blaze on the 30th of November 2012 with a statistical significance at the 95% level. This is particularly significant as CJ was the first publicly traded firm, and one of the first firms to enter the market, setting the stage for the widespread growth eSports s experiences today. Furthermore, this date has a positive coefficient signifying the positive reactions investors had to this event. Other player transfers that were statistically significant were the departures of Ambition and Coco as well as the acquisition Cain and Reach on the 30th of November 2012, a move viewed by many as the long needed overhaul CJ's long underperforming roster and coaching staff. Statistically significant tournaments placements were the Season 2 Regional finals on the 12th of September 2012, IEM Season 7 on September 16th 2012, IEM season 9 on the 14th of March 2015 and the SBENU Champion Summer 2015. These events were all significant at the 90% level except for the IEM Season 9 tournament, which had a 95% confidence level. What makes IEM cologne unique is that it is one of first large scale international tournaments that CJ participated in, essentially, their first international brand exposure in the League of Legends scene. Their loss to European team Fnatic in the semi-finals of the tournament could have been reflected in the negative coefficient of abnormal returns as many local investors likely anticipated a higher finish on CJs first international endeavours.

The results discovered with a 30 day estimation window mirrored the 15 day estimation windows except for a loss of confidence from a 95% level to a 90% level for the Season 2 Regional Finals, the SBENU champions' summer 2015 and the creation of CJ's first line-up. However, what is interesting to note is that, the rule enacted on the 28th of October 2014 disallowing the use of Sister Teams, and thus forcing CJ to merge their rosters into a single line-up, develops a statistical significance at the 90% level when tested with a 30 day estimation window. This is perhaps due to the fact that many perceived this change to have weakened the Korean region as Sister teams were an integral part of Korean infrastructure, allowing any team to practice new strategies behind closed doors, training against their counterparts, however, both of CJs rosters were significantly underperforming. This change perhaps allowed some to hope that CJ would acquire some new talent in the form of those to be displaced from their current rosters.

Together, these results suggest that there could possibly be a non-definitive correlation between tournament placement, important roster changes and eSports team sponsorship onto the share prices of the corporation.   Utilising an estimation window of 15 days, only three events were statistically significant. At the 90% confidence level, only the 6th place finish in the SBENU champions' summer 2015 on the 7th of August 2015 was significant. The 95% level highlights two events, The 2nd place finish in the 2015 Season Korea Regional finals on the 9th of May 2015 and the Rule Change disallowing the use of sister teams. The significance of the 2015 playoff success was likely highly significant due to the rather poor season run with Jin Air finishing in 6th, barely qualifying for the finals before embarking on a miraculous run through the gauntlet, finally only falling at the Grand Finals and narrowly missing out on the last seed for the 2015 World Finals. Once again the rule change of the 28th October 2014 has a statistically significant impact on Korean Air share prices though, unlike the CJ case, this change has a negative coefficient.

Concerning the 30 day window, whilst the Rule change remains consistently significant, as does the 2nd place finish in the 2015 Korean Regional finals, however Jin Air's 6th place finish in the summer season of 2015 loses its significance. However, Jin Air's 5th place finish in the SK Telecom LTE-A LOL Masters 2014 became significant at the 90% level. However, what must be noted about the Jin Air results is that the effects of events on the price and shares of the Jin Air Green Wings will be diluted. This is as mentioned in my methodology, the share prices of Korean air were used to approximate share price reactions of Jin Air, a subsidiary of Korean air.

Applying a 15 day estimation window, the Kt Corporation's bullet's second place finish in the HOT6ix Champions Summer 2013 on the 31st of August 2013 was significant at the 95% confidence interval. Three events were significant at the 99% confidence interval, Kt's second place finish in the SBENU Champions Summer 2015 on the 29th of August 2015, the 5-th place finish in the 2015 Season World Championship on the 18th of October 2015 and the rule change of the 28th of October 2014. When approximating the abnormal return with a 30 day estimation window, results were similar except that Kt's finish the HOT6ix Champions Summer 2013 became increasingly significant, rising to the 99% confidence level.

Once again, the rule change was statistically significant across both estimation windows. Kt's second place finish in the SBENU Champions summer 2015 was significant as they completed the season having performed greater than expected. The effects of this season may have been diluted as the season implied a campaign lasting approximately 2 months. However, despite their strong showing at the Regional finals, their poor showing at the world championships, did not signify a negative share price shift as one would expect, showing a coefficient of 0.193.

Samsung's results of a 15 day estimation window, showed a surprising lack of statistical significance in Samsung White's crowning as world champions on the 19th of October 2014 whilst Samsung White's triumph over their sister team, Samsung Blue in the semi-finals of the same World Championship was significant to the 99% confidence level with a coefficient of 2.161. Samsung's 7th place finish in the SBENU Champions Summer 2015 was also statistically significant and has a positive coefficient despite having a low overall placement. The rule change was once again statistically significant at the 99% level with a positive coefficient as well as Samsung's announcement of their new roster on the 2nd of December 2014. However, unlike other sponsors, at this point in time, Samsung were sponsoring two of the top four teams in the world, coupled with the fact that the new line-up announced was relatively underwhelming, the positive coefficient is rather perplexing. For the 30 day estimation windows, much of the results were similar, barring the loss in significance of Samsung white's victory over their sister team Samsung Blue in the World Championship Semi-finals, which is now significant at the 95% level.

Observing the results of a 15 day estimation windows on SK telecom showed that although the formation of SKT's initial roster was not statistically significant, the creation of their second roster on the 28th of February 2013, SKT T1 K was statistically significant at the 99% level, albeit with a negative coefficient. This may be due to the fact that almost the entirety of K's roster was composed of amateurs, essentially unknown quantities in the scene. Though it must be noted that as time passed, these rookies quickly grew into their own, becoming some of the game's most iconic players. K's victory over the Korean Regional finals on the 7th of September and eventual crowning as World Champions on the 4th of October 2013 were also statistically significant, however, the World Finals victory had a negative coefficient was surprising especially considering how the team swept the competition,

Another event of statistical significance at the 99% level was the departure of Piglet and PoohManDu, two members of SKT's World Championship winning line-up, on the 17th of September 2014, where the team had a dreadful season, failing to even qualify for the World Championships and attempt a defence of their title. However, the departure of another member of their World Championship winning team 3 months later, Impact, was not statistically significant perhaps due to his relatively lacklustre play during the twilight of his time on the SKT roster. Finally, after a yearlong hiatus from the world stage, SKT reclaimed their title as World Champions on the 31st of October 2015, an event with a coefficient of 1.417 and a confidence level of 99%. Shortly after reclaiming the title, team captain, and widely regarded as the greatest League of Legends player of all time, Lee "Faker" Sang-hyeok re-signed his contract with SK telecom for the 2016 season. The event had a confidence level of 99% and a positive coefficient of 0.323 signifying investor's perception in the importance of retaining the iconic Korean superstar.

When observing events with a 30 day estimation window, the results were largely similar barring a loss in confidence concerning the departure of Piglet and PoohManDu on the 17th of September 2014, an event now having only a 95% level of statistical significance. Furthermore, the coefficient of the K's victory during the 2013 World Championships not only remained consistent with a 99% confidence interval but also had a positive coefficient when regressed onto the share prices of SK telecom. Taking these two sets of results together, there appears to be a correlation between SKTs success, particularly at the absolute highest level of competition and the fluctuations of their share prices. Furthermore, relative to other teams, SKT share prices seem to be much more largely impacted by the transfer of players. This is likely as every impactful transfer involved a player of SKT's world championship winning roster in 2013.

It is important to note that the rule change on the 28th of October 2014 held no significance to the SKT organisation, perhaps due to the overwhelming success of SKT T1 K and their title as reigning world champions, the question of which players would stay and which would leave were rather apparent.

As a whole, the results indicate, an admittedly inconsistent, correlation between League of Legends events and the share prices of owning corporations. In particular, a large number of large scale international tournaments finishes were deemed to be statistically significant. Examples of this include CJ's 3-4th place finish at IEM 7, Samsung White's victory over sister team Samsung Blue during the 2014 World Championships or SKT's two World Championship victories. This is likely due to the perceived benefits of an increase in brand exposure for these Korean firms at a large scale international level.

The beginning of a sponsorship deal by a major corporation failed to yield many significant results with the exception of the CJ Corporation's foray into the League of Legends scene, likely as it is the first such venture into a rapidly growing, but unknown, factor. Furthermore, player transfers seem to be held in the regard that only players of the highest quality seem to have any impact on share prices. Examples of this includes the resigning of "Faker" on SKT or the departure of Ambition and Coco from CJ Entus. Surprisingly, some players such as Jin Air's control midlaner 'GBM" or Kt's super star top laner Yoon "Maknoon" Ha-Woon did not impact share prices at a statistically significant level.

The rule change enacted on the 28th of October 2014 was a statistically significant impact at the 99% level for firms such as the Jin Air, the Kt Corporation and Samsung electronics. One reason for this is that during the 2014 season, all three of these teams were struggling to compete even at a domestic level. As such, the rule change opened up the possibility of stealing talent from other organizations so as to bolster their own rosters. Unfortunately, as reflected in CJ Entus's share price returns, most of these players were poached by foreign regions such as China and the West who were simply willing to pay more for top tier talent. Kt Rolster's new roster announcement following this change was also nearly statistically significant with a t value of -1.624 with a 15 day estimation window and a coefficient of -0.001.The rule change also had no impact on the share prices of SK telecom perhaps due to the loyalty of players such as "Faker" who reportedly declined contracts valued up to $1 million by Chinese sides (Jou, 2014).

Conclusion

This goal of this thesis was to ascertain whether or not a League of Legends team's success, player transfer dealings or failure has a quantifiable effect on the share price returns of their main sponsoring corporation.

The results indicate that, for the most part, the transfer of players and the beginning of a sponsorship lacked statistical significance. However, there seems to exist a relationship between these events and the owning corporation. Specifically, for increasingly prestigious tournaments boasting not only an enormous prize pool but, perhaps more importantly an ever growing viewer base. Examples of these large scale events include SBENU Champions Summer or the annual World Championships.

On the other hand, significant alterations of rules such as allowing a firm to sponsor one team was, in most cases, statistically significant. One reason for this is the elimination of sister teams prompted other corporations into the industry to seize the opportunity to pick up the additional left over talent who were unrestrained by their original organization. This significantly altered the landscape of the Korean League of Legend scene's infrastructure within the sport.

Moreover, results were in accordance with that of previous research, for example, Brown and Hartzell (2001) or Kim (2015) in showing that the performances of a sponsored team will have a statistically significant impact on the share price returns of a sponsoring corporation. Furthermore, data corroborated with Edmans et Al. (2007) when they discovered that events of increasing importance, such as the World Championships, have a larger effect on share price returns. Kamakura (1995), suggested that celebrity endorsements contracts have a positive effect on share price returns. This is evidenced in the increase of share price returns following talent acquisition and tournament success as tournament winners become celebrities in Korea whilst the acquisition of a well-known player is always a positive influence on a team's brand.

As such, while owning corporations benefit from both the brand exposure an Esports stream provides as well as the celebrity endorsements of the players on the team, these teams benefit from the monetary support and infrastructure the sponsoring corporations provide them. As such the common misconception that purchasing and running a sports team is merely a symbol of prestige, will hopefully begin to dispel as results of the Korean League of Legends eSports scene shows that owning corporations should consider increasing investment into the scene as there exists a quantifiable mutually beneficial scenario for both firm and team.

Filbert Goetomo grew up in Jakarta, Indonesia and is a recent graduate of Claremont Mckenna College's class of 2016 with a bachelor's degree in Economics. Raised around computers and consoles, his interests lie in tech, finance and competitive gaming. He views competitive gaming as the future of both entertainment and athletics. He currently works as for Grab Indonesia. He occasionally writes for Gosu-Gamers and also enjoys reading fantasy novels and playing football.

References

Base Menu. (n.d.). Retrieved March 25, 2016, from http://www.CJ.co.kr/CJ-en/company/investor/financial;jsessionid=5DA1AD0C0B31EF23FBCC215B5B30FFD8

Breslau, R. (2012). League of Legends Season 2 Championships most watched Esports event of all time. Retrieved April 18, 2016, from http://www.gamespot.com/articles/league-of-legends-season-2-championships-most-watched-Esports s-event-of-all-time/1100-6398663/

Brown, G. & Hartzell, J. (2001). "Market reaction to public information: The atypical case of the Boston Celtics," Journal of Financial Economics, Eslevier, vol. 60, pages 333-370, May.

Brown, S. J., & Warner, J. B. (1980). Measuring Security Price Performance. Retrieved April 25, 2016, from http://www.simon.rochester.edu/fac/warner/Jerry Papers/JFE-September 80.pdf

Casselman, B. (2015). Resistance is futile: Esports s is massive ... and growing. Retrieved March 16, 2016, from http://espn.go.com/espn/story/_/id/13059210/Esports s-massive-industry-growing

Coates, D. &. Humphreys, B. R. (2008). "The Effect of On-Field Success on Stock Prices: Evidence from Nippon Professional Baseball," Working Papers 0805, International Association of Sports Economists; North American Association of Sports Economists

Consolidated Financial Statements of Samsung electronics Co., Ltd. And Subsidiaries (2016, February 25). Retrieved March 22, 2016, from http://www.samsung.com/us/aboutsamsung/investor_relations/financial_information/downloads/2015/2015_con_quarter04_all.pdf

Daniel, J. (2013). Shell, Glencore, and Other Multinationals Dominate Their Home Economies. Retrieved March 23, 2016, from http://www.bloomberg.com/news/articles/2013-04-04/shell-glencore-and-other-multinationals-dominate-their-home-economies

Deesing, J. (2014). Korean Professional League Getting Overhauled. Retrieved March 30, 2016, from http://www.redbull.com/us/en/Esports s/stories/1331687251385/korean-professional-league-getting-overhauled

Deesing, J. (2014). Samsung White and Blue Torn Apart by Roster Swaps. Retrieved March 30, 2016, from http://www.redbull.com/us/en/Esports s/stories/1331688668203/samsung-white-and-blue-torn-apart-by-roster-swaps

Dreunen, J. V. (2015). Esports The Market Breif 2015. Retrieved March 13, 2016, from http://www.snjv.org/wp-content/uploads/2015/05/Esports s_Market_Brief_2015_SuperData_Research.pdf

Edmans, A., Garcia, D., & Norli, Ø. (August 27). The Journal of FinanceVolume 62, Issue 4, Article first published online: 14 AUG 2007. Retrieved April 24, 2016, from http://onlinelibrary.wiley.com/doi/10.1111/j.1540-6261.2007.01262.x/pdf

Edwards, T. F. (2013). Esports: A Brief History | Gaming | ADANAI. Retrieved March 12, 2016, from http://adanai.com/Esports s/

Figueira, M. (2015). The viewership of the 2015 League of Legends World Championship toppled Riot's expectations. Retrieved April 18, 2016, from http://www.lazy-gamer.net/genre/moba/viewership-2015-league-legends-world-championship-toppled-riots-expectations/

Kamakura, W. A. (1995). The Economic Worth of Celebrity Endorsers: An Event Study Analysis. Retrieved April 24, 2016, from http://papers.ssrn.com/sol3/papers.cfm?abstract_id=2424837

Kim, M. J. (2015). "Money Craving in China and Korea: Football Club Performance and the Share Prices of Owning Corporations". CMC Senior Theses. Paper 1044. http://scholarship.claremont.edu/cmc_theses/1044

Korean Air Lines Co., Ltd. And It's Subsidiaries. (2015). Retrieved March 24, 2016, from https://www.koreanair.com/content/dam/koreanair/en/documents/AboutKoreanAir/InvestorRelations/FinancialStatements/Korean_Air_2014_Financial_Statements.pdf

KT corporation and Subsidiaries Consolidated Financial Statements. (n.d.). Retrieved March 23, 2016, from http://quote.morningstar.com/stock-filing/Other/2015/12/31/t.aspx?t=:KT

L. (2015). Home Grown Talent, A Deeper Look at Korean Esports s Glory. Retrieved April 18, 2016, from https://gamurs.com/articles/home-grown-talent-a-deeper-look-at-korean-Esports s-glory

Lewis, R. (2014). Azubu is about to give Korea's Esports s stars their own streaming platform. Retrieved March 30, 2016, from http://www.dailydot.com/Esports s/azubu-kespa-deal/

Mackinlay, C. (1997). Event Studies in Economics and Finance. Retrieved April 18, 2016, from http://www.jstor.org/stable/2729691?seq=1#page_scan_tab_contents

McCormick, R. (2013). 'League of Legends' Esports finals watched by 32 million people. Retrieved April 18, 2016, from http://www.theverge.com/2013/11/19/5123724/league-of-legends-world-championship-32-million-viewers

Most played PC games 2015 | Statistic. (2016). Retrieved March 13, 2016, from http://www.statista.com/statistics/251222/most-played-pc-games/

NewsWorld .NOVEMBER 2006. (n.d.). Retrieved March 22, 2016, from http://nw.newsworld.co.kr/cont/article2009/0905-60.htm

P., & Jou, E. (2014). Top League of Legends Player Worth Close To $1 Million. Retrieved April 25, 2016, from http://kotaku.com/top-league-of-legends-player-worth-close-to-1-million-1653937237

Peterson, U. (2015). Lol summoner rift jungle map Powered by RebelMouse. Retrieved March 16, 2016, from https://www.rebelmouse.com/uhasegopeterson/lol-summoner-rift-jungle-map-1294574973.html

Reiser, M., Breuer, C., & Wicker, P. (2012). The Sponsorship Effect: Do Sport Sponsorship Announcements Impact the Firm Value of Sponsoring Firms? Retrieved April 24, 2016, from http://www98.griffith.edu.au/dspace/bitstream/handle/10072/48706/82048_1.pdf?sequence=1

Schwartz, N. (2014). More people watch Esports s than watch the World Series or NBA Finals. Retrieved April 18, 2016, from http://ftw.usatoday.com/2014/05/league-of-legends-popularity-world-series-nba

SK Telecom Co., Ltd. (2014). Annual Report 2014. Retrieved March 22, 2016, from http://asia.cdn.euroland.com/arinhtml/KR-SKM/2014/AR_ENG_2014/index.htm

So- Hyun, K. (2013). [Power Korea] CJ rises as beacon of Korean food, shopping, pop culture. Retrieved March 25, 2016, from http://www.koreaherald.com/view.php?ud=20130304000759

Sun-Young, L. (2008). Mobile operators pressured to cut call, message rates. Retrieved March 22, 2016, from http://news.naver.com/main/read.nhn?mode=LPOD&mid=sec&sid1=&oid=044&aid=0000070179

Tran, E. (2012). The Time Has Come: League of Legends' Impact on the Rapid Growth of Esports - IGN. Retrieved April 11, 2016, from http://www.ign.com/articles/2012/10/17/the-time-has-come-riots-impact-on-the-rapid-growth-of-Esports s

Young, D. (2015). Why is Korea so good at Esports? - Ebuyer Blog. Retrieved April 24, 2016, from http://www.ebuyer.com/blog/2015/10/why-is-korea-so-good-at-Esports s/

Ergonomics and Videogames: Habits, Diseases and Health Perception of Gamers

By Christian Esteban Martín Luján

Ergonomics has traditionally been described as the study of equipment designed for the workplace. Nowadays, this term has been expanded to all those situations where artefacts are designed for a general use. There are different kinds of ergonomics. The most well-known is physical ergonomics, where posture is primarily involved. This means that every environmental part of the workstation has to be designed to help the posture be as natural and healthy as possible, even if people are sitting or standing. There are other kinds of ergonomics, such as psychological or cognitive ergonomics, which considers the stimulus people receive from their environment, their interaction with their co-workers, the complexity of decisions to take, and so on (Canas & Waerns, 2001).

Since computers are mostly seen as working accessories or entertainment, many papers have been written about how ergonomics can help in the office or ordinary life. Back pain has been the most studied problem because of its importance concerning posture when using the computer.

The majority of researchers have based their studies on different aspects of posture hygiene, coming to conclusions such as how vibrations in the lower back could help on long sitting situations, where back support and hand support were found to be important factors due to posture (M-Pranesh et al., 2010). Other studies have focused on the action of constant rotatory movements in the lower back of the chair, which demonstrated promising results, reducing lower back pain, while not being disturbing to work (van Deursen et al., 1999). It has also been studied how proper support to the pelvic area helps long sitting patients, confirming a decrease of lumbar flattening by using a pillow as lumbar support (Grondin et al., 2013).

How the hamstring is related to lower back pain in computer-related workers has also been researched, where prolonged sitting was found to change the normal pattern of hamstring muscle activity (Kim & Yoo, 2013).

There is a paper on how the lower back responds to different chairs and positions that states that the Balance® Multi-Chair promotes a more natural lumbar curvature and causes less lumbar flexion. The chair is designed with a forward-tilted seat for a thigh-trunk angle of about 120 degrees to preserve the normal lumbar lordosis, as it has been found that this causes less lumbar flexion in subjects writing at a desk. This seat is believed to be an appropriate adjunct to patient care when less flexion or slight extension of the lumbar spine is indicated in the sitting position (Frey & Tecklin, 1986).

It has also been looked into whether reclining a chair really helps with the different curves of the body (cervical, dorsal, lumbar). It has been verified that all intervertebral discs move relative to one another after a change in seating posture. Although the positions in this particular article were defined by the shape of the backrest, high inter-subject variability of the shape of the upper spinal segments has been observed for the sitting positions. Dynamic seating options are considered to play a key role in maintaining spinal health, especially in subjects with desk jobs (Zemp et al., 2013).

The upper extremities have also been found to be highly affected by the use of computers. How different keyboards affect the upper limbs has also been considered, and it has been concluded that specific designs for keyboards give a more natural posture (Baker & Cidboy, 2006).

Continuing in relation to computers, the relationship between mouse use and musculoskeletal symptoms, such as neck and wrist discomfort, has been investigated; finding that mouse use constitutes an additional risk factor for musculoskeletal symptoms, particularly relating to the arm posture adopted (Cook et al., 2000). The risk computer-related jobs have for the forearm has also been considered, and it has been pointed out that mouse use is the biggest risk factor for forearm pain (Kryger, 2003).

Even though it is known that a huge part of lower back problems come from prolonged sitting positions (Lis et al., 2006), it is interesting to note that these problems can come from multiple other factors, and not only from prolonged sitting (Bener et al. 2014). Change in the pattern of shoulder and pelvic coordination is known to affect subjects with recurrent lower back pain. It is believed that clinicians need to consider gender differences in kinematic strategies during trunk axial rotation to cope with underlying problems in subjects with recurrent lower back pain (Park et al., 2012).

This question highlights the fact that the global exploration of the impact that computers have in the health of the population is still under-studied, and additional factors such as keyboards, mice, or controllers should be taken more into account. To our knowledge, only an isolated research about how computers can affect the eye has been published, which clearly found a connection between computer use and eye damage (Logaraj et al., 2014).

Returning to the matter of ergonomics, relatively few studies have been made about the importance of the application of this science to computer or console gaming. It has been pointed out that ergonomic consulting is beneficial alongside other techniques for the neck and shoulder region, even though by itself, it is equally effective (Voerman et al., 2007). It has also been noted that interaction between physiotherapists who are specialized in ergonomics, and computer-related workers is very beneficial in decreasing discomfort and musculoskeletal strain and pain, even more so than only educating the workers in ergonomics (Ketola et al., 2002). Another point of view has been studied, focusing on the creation of an algorithm that can predict the joint movements (Wang, 1999). This algorithm can be used to reduce injuries by applying it to the ergonomic design of computer or console accessories such as the mouse, keyboard, or controller.

Since the sitting position is the one that gamers use most, it is of use to know that supported arm conditions while sitting reduces lumbar stress (Occhipinti, 1986). There is also evidence that the inclination of the desk can affect the posture of the individual, 10 degrees being known to have the effect of improving the neck and trunk posture (de Wall et al., 1992).

Specific postural training has been demonstrated to be very important to activate stabilizing muscles while sitting, lumbo-sacral stabilizers being the most crucial. There is evidence that different upright sitting postures result in different trunk muscle activation patterns. When compared to lumbo-pelvic upright sitting, thoracic upright sitting has been defined by increased thoracic lordosis, less lumbar lordosis, and less anterior pelvic tilt. In turn, these results were associated with greater activation of the thoracic erector spine and the external oblique, and reduced the superficial lumbar multifidus and the internal oblique activation, leading to the conclusion that postural training is necessary for a healthier back posture (O´Sullivan et al., 2006).

It has been also pointed out that sitting back with both feet placed on a rest and using aired or slow foam cushions reduces the pressure on the seat surface (Defloor & Grypdonck, 1999). Also neck and shoulder pains have been related to lordotic lumbo-pelvic postures rather than cervicothoracic postures while sitting (Straker et al., 2009).

Despite this extensive knowledge, the role of ergonomics in Electronic Sports (eSports) has not been explored yet. There is not yet an official definition of eSports, but it can easily be compared to any professional sport such as football, basketball, and others. What characterises eSports is a high number of people playing for long hours via computer or console to achieve the goal of becoming a professional videogame player, which if they succeed, would imply more hours dedicated to training for real tournaments. Since the first console was released up until May 2014, 140 million consoles have been sold (Statista, 2015). This data implies a high number of people sitting in sofas or chairs playing many hours with different controllers for which there are no available studies. The only console study that has been reported is about the Wii console, which is a review of different accidents described in a web site, and its conclusion just states that Wii injuries are not rare, and the most common injuries are hand lacerations and/or bruising, attributed to the interface of the console (pcgamer.com, 2014).

The impact videogames are having in the worldwide population can be illustrated by the following graphics of active eSports users in Europe from March 2014 until February 2015.

In the graphic below we present a year's worth of statistics of how many people are playing in the Electronic Sports League competitions per day, which in April 2014 reached around 80,000 players in just one day.

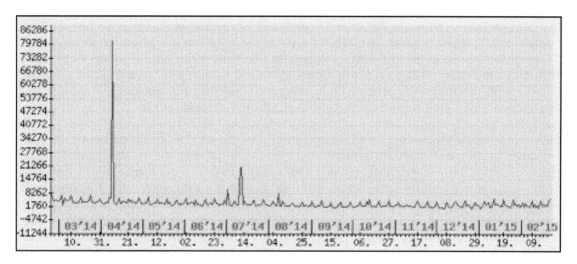

Figure 1: Matches per day in the Electronic Sports League in Europe

The next graphic quantifies the number of matches that have been played in a year, which reaches about 22,540,000 between February 2014 and February 2015.

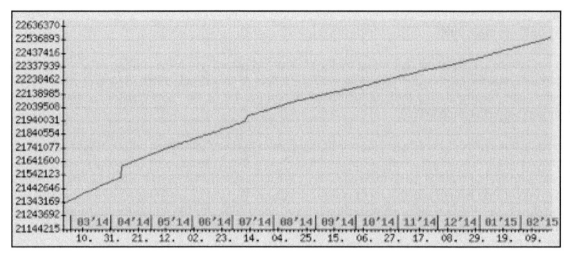

Figure 2: Total Matches in a year in the Electronic Sports League in Europe

To continue the justification of the study, it is important to know that over 2.2 million players play Counter Strike [a first person shooter video game] monthly (pcgamer.com, 2014) and 67 million play League of Legends [an internet multiplayer game] monthly (Forbes, 2013). Moreover, a study claims that 59% of the population of the United States plays videogames (theesa.com, 2014).

Such is the importance of people playing eSports that the United States government has accepted eSports gamers as professional athletes (Forbes, 2015). Even more, universities in the Unites States have started to give scholarships to students with outstanding gaming skills (Forbes, 2015).

It has also been pointed out that sedentary activities, such as television-related activities, increase health risks (Shephard, 2012; Helajärvi, 2014). And even though the quantity of activity is not yet established, it is known that physical activity decreases death risks (Gonzales-Gross & Melendez, 2013). There is even proof that exercise is, metabolically speaking, effective in improving general health (Ringseis et al., 2015). Other studies reveal that it is not necessary to exercise outside work: even if the job is based on sitting in front a computer, you can exercise by using a sitting-standing workstation that reduces sitting time, and potentially improve your health (Chau et al., 2014; Dutta et al., 2014).

Due to the growing importance of the gaming industry, it seems logical to think that as part of the health community, physiotherapists should be more conscious of the health risks this area can bring. We should start considering how to prevent these problems and treat them. We will soon be facing a large number patients referring to symptoms we are not familiar with because they still haven't been given the attention they need, and we must prepare for this. It is important for physiotherapists to begin studying the possibility that we will have to be present at eSports stadiums as part of the gaming teams as much as we are part of football, basketball, or any other kind of sports team. We also have to prepare ourselves to give advice to keep gamers away from repeating the same injuries they could be exposed to. It is possible that most of the problems will come from repetitive strain injuries, vision problems, postural injuries, and sedentary related diseases. This is our area and if it is demonstrated that these injuries are relevant, we must be prepared to face them.

The first step is to analyse which are the most common injuries in this kind of user and try to identify the principal sources they come from. It is important for us to learn to interpret the reasons the lesions are made and how we can help to avoid them.

Objectives and hypothesis

Objectives

This study has several objectives. First, this study will try to examine the gaming habits of players. Specifically, we want to know the percentage of people who prefer computer videogames against those who prefer consoles, and how often they play.

The second objective of this study is to analyse which kinds of diseases are more frequent in the general sample, and also as a function of type of player: sex, time spent playing, and physical activity.
With complementary stats we will try to define whether accessory tools are useful in avoiding specific ailments, such as type of seat, type of keyboard and mouse, type of table, and supplementary objects that should help with the ergonomics.

Finally, we will try to determine which the most painful parts of the body are for gamers and which could be the causes of those injuries.

Hypothesis

From a physiotherapeutic point of view, the problems most likely to be found are with the neck, shoulders, and back. This is due to the sitting position and the type of chair or table, which will force the stabilizing muscles to act more than they should, causing them to contract, possibly resulting in casual pain. Other possible injuries could be a result of repetitive strain injury caused by the impact of the fingers against the mouse or keyboard, most likely if they don't have specific gaming accessories. Compression on the wrist could cause carpal tunnel, which leads to various hand problems.

The sedentary lifestyle can bring also many muscle problems, such as tendon shortening, strength loss, fatigue, and other problems that will give rise to painful situations in any part of the body, such as pressure, bloodstream problems, obesity, and so on.

Taking into account these aspects, we propose the following hypothesis:
1. Computer players will have more wrist problems than console players.
2. Console players will have more back and neck problems than computer players.
3. Those who play more often will have more pains in general.
4. Those with vision problems will have more headaches.
5. Those who use armchairs or sofa will have more back and neck problems than those who use chairs.
6. Active players will feel healthier than sedentary players.

Methods

Participants

There are a total of 93 game players in the survey, with an average age of 24.34. 66% are men and 32% are women. Also 95.7% are not professional players, against the 4.3% who are professional players.

Materials

A questionnaire was designed to retrieve as much information as possible from players online. Google Forms® was used to develop the survey. To analyse the data, SPSS® 1.9 statistics package was used. The tables and charts were created in Microsoft Office Excel 2010®.

The survey designed was very specific so that only regular videogame players could answer it; giving them options that only those who are familiar with the matter could answer.

The first part of the questionnaire covered the basic information of the subjects, such as sex or age, to set the base of the study.

The next part of the survey tried to narrow down the relationship of the subjects with videogames, asking whether they were professional videogame players, if they preferred computer or console, and which kind of computer (none, desktop computer, or laptop computer) and console (none, Xbox, PlayStation, or Wii) they used. They were also asked about the days (1 day per week, 2/3 days per week, 4/5 days per week, Daily) and hours per day (0 hours, 1 to 4 hours, 5 to 8 hours, more than 8 hours) they spent playing, and device (computer or console) used. This way we can slide the variables and focus on particular aspects.

In the following section, we included a question about how often (1. Never, 2. Occasionally, 3. Sometimes, 4. Frequently, 5. Daily) some parts of their bodies hurt, the parts being Head, Neck, Shoulder, Elbow, Wrist, Finger, Back, Hip, Leg, Knee, and Ankle, and additional questions about which body parts hurt while playing, if they have vision problems while playing, and whether they need visual support.

Afterwards we tried to figure out what their ergonomic furniture and accessories were. Questions such as what kind of table they use (Trestle board, Desk, Specific computer desk, Standard table), if they sit on a chair or a sofa, the specifics of the chair (is it adjustable in height; can it recline; does it have lumbar support; does It have head support; does it have armrests; does it have wheels), whether they have a footrest, and the type of keyboard and mouse they use (standard or gaming). This way we can understand better where the origin of the problem could be.

The fifth set of questions is useful to assess the lifestyle of the subjects. They were questioned about their physical activity habits, how many days per week and hours per day (options as above) they spent exercising and pauses taken (No pauses, I rest after every game/round/fight, I rest once an hour, I can spend more than two hours without resting, I only stop when something hurts) between games, rounds, or fights.

Lastly they were asked to evaluate their health status (1. Really bad, 2. Bad, 3. Normal, 4. Good, 5. Excellent). This will allow us to verify whether what they answered before and what they feel like concurs or not.

Design and Procedure

The questionnaire was launched through the internet via social networks such as Facebook and Twitter in Spain.

Once the number of survey responses was sufficient for meaningful analysis, the questionnaire was closed from Google Forms® and the statistical analysis started.

Data Analysis

The first block was dedicated to the playing habits of the gamers in a descriptive analysis.

The next block considered injuries and health perception. The average amount of pain felt in each body part was compared between those who play on computer and those who play on console. Afterwards we compared the same items with the variable of types of pain while playing. A table with the average responses of the most common type of pain, with the standard deviation, was also put in the study.

The next step in this block was to compare groups in the sample. The tables had the number of subjects, the average and standard deviation of each item and the variance between groups (F), and the significance (where <0.05 is significant, but taking at least <0.085 as potentially significant) of the variables' datum. First, gender was considered, then the type of console they use, whether they exercise or not, if they need visual support, and how many days a week they play. The computer and console players, and the hours per day they played, were also studied but were not detailed in this paper.

Results

Playing Habits

We found that 71% of the subjects preferred to play with computers, while the other 29% preferred to play with consoles. Concerning this data, we found that 70.5% of men preferred computers against 29.5% who preferred consoles. Women preferred computers as well, which represented 71.9% in comparison to the 28.1% who preferred consoles. The data analysis shows that most participants preferred playing with computers than with consoles, with the same proportions when the preferences of men and women were studied.

Following a general description of the sample, we found that 2.2% of the subjects didn't play with any kind of computer, 44.1% played with laptop computers, and 53.8% of the players used desktop computers. On the other hand, 32.3% didn't use any type of console, 37.6% preferred PlayStation, 16.1% played Xbox, and 14% played Wii. This highlights that desktop computers are the most used and that PlayStation or no console at all where the most common choices.

Figure 3shows the days per week the subjects play video games. The highest portion of people played every day, this being 43% of the players. As we go on, it can be seen that 22% of the participants played 2 or 3 days per week, 20% played in between 4 and 5 days, and in the smallest group we have 15% playing 1 day per week. This time of exposure to computers and consoles could be compared with part-time jobs.

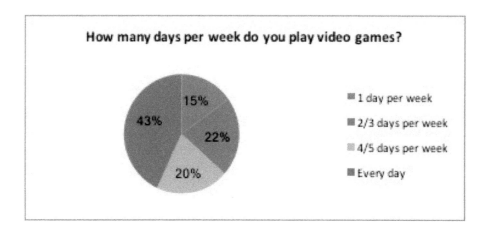

Figure 3: Days per week gamers play

Figure 4 and 5 show percentages of players divided into hours played per day, so that we can see how many of them play as much as a work shift, between those who play console or computer.

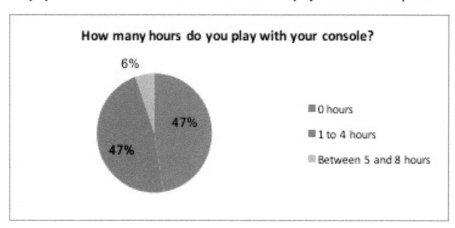

Figure 4: Hours per day gamers play console videogames

The same amount of console subjects plays 0 hours or between 1 and 4 hours, which is 47% for each. The other 6% lies between 5 and 8 hours. In this specific data stat, none of the console players spend more than 8 hours playing.

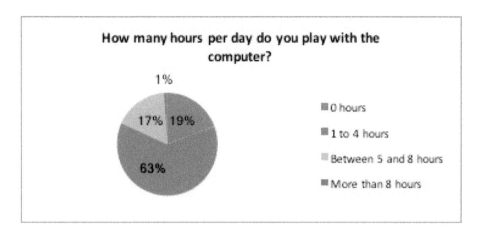

Figure 5: Hours per day gamers play computer videogames

Computer players have a more determined preference, where 63% of the participants play from 1 to 4 hours. Those who do not play at all with computers represent 19% of the answers. Another 17% play between 5 to 8 hours. Only 1% play for more than 8 hours.

This time of exposure to computers and consoles could be compared with part-time jobs.

Injuries and health perception

With this data we have the basis of our study, which will now lead us to the most important part of this research: the most common ailments found depending on different factors.

In Figure 6 we present the average amount of pain that gamers usually feel in each part of the body for the entire sample, those who play on computers, and those who play on consoles.

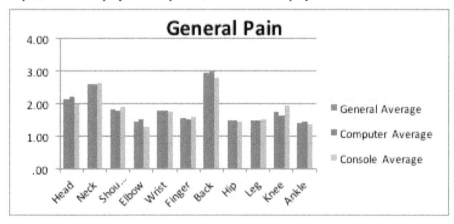

Figure 6: Pain felt in different body normally parts by the whole sample, computer sample, and console sample

The chart shows that the back is the most painful body part, followed by the neck for the three variables, responses moving between occasionally and sometimes. Then we can see that computer players have more pain related to the head, suffering from it more than occasionally, while console players have more pain in the knee, suffering from it almost occasionally. The rest of the variables are less commonly suffered and are relatively even between the two kinds of users. This suggests that players suffer from back and neck pain more frequently than from pain in other parts of the body, which is consistent with the fact that most of the articles focus on these problems for computer users.

Figure 7 explains the relationship between the body part where people feel pain when they are playing and the type of device they use. It also includes the whole sample.

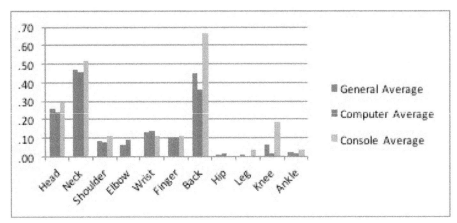

Figure 7: Pain felt in different body parts while playing by the whole sample, computer sample, and console sample

As can be seen, console players have more pain related to the back than computer players. Neck problems are the second most common body part which suffers in their game time. Computer players, on the other hand, experience much less pain while playing, the neck being the most common problem and the back the second most. This continues the trend the research articles had, and confirms that the back and neck are the body parts most affected by videogames.

Complementarily to the charts, Figure 8 presents the average and standard deviation for the types of pain in regular bases, which confirms again what has already been said.

How often do you feel pain in these body parts?		
	Average	St. Dev.
Head	2,13	,969
Neck	2,60	1,143
Shoulder	1,82	1,083
Elbow	1,45	,787
Wrist	1,77	,934
Finger	1,54	,891
Back	2,94	1,140

Hip	1,46	,916
Leg	1,49	,761
Knee	1,73	1,095
Ankle	1,42	,876

Figure 8: Average and standard deviation of pain assiduousness.

Figure 9 shows how participants consider their health situation.

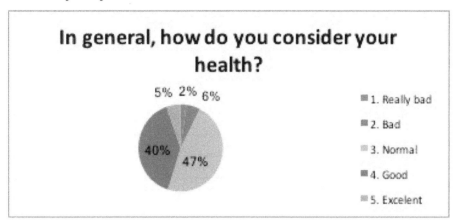

Figure 9: Self health consideration by the whole sample

Most of the players, 47%, believe they are in normal health. The next group is made up of 40% of participants, and they consider that they are in good health. Only 6% think they are in bad health and 2% that they are in really bad health. The last 5% corresponds to those who think that their health is excellent.

4.3 Comparisons between groups

Different mean comparisons were carried out, using ANOVA, in order to determine if there were statistical differences in the amount of pain that gamers suffered in each body part studied, as well as their general health perception.

When we compared console and computer gamers, we found that there were no significant differences between the afflictions reported. There were also no differences in concern with the hours played. No significance was found for the type of mouse or keyboard used either. For that reason, we decided not to put the tables in this part of the study.

In relation to the perception of pain depending on gender, we found significance in perception of headache and shoulder pain, which affected more of the female gender than the male gender, as can be seen in Figure 10. This could be explained by the fact that women and men play with different habits and routines; however, more research would be needed to confirm and understand this result.

	Men Pain (n=61)		Women Pain (n=32)			
Pain	Average	St. Dev	Average	St. Dev	F	Sig.
Head	1,98	,940	2,41	,979	4,125	**,045**
Neck	2,49	1,105	2,81	1,203	1,663	,200
Shoulder	1,54	,828	2,34	1,310	13,044	**,000**
Elbow	1,44	,786	1,47	,803	,023	,880
Wrist	1,75	,907	1,81	,988	,081	,776
Finger	1,57	,957	1,47	,761	,289	,592
Back	2,87	1,103	3,06	1,216	,603	,440
Hip	1,44	,866	1,50	1,016	,082	,776
Leg	1,44	,719	1,59	,837	,827	,366
Knee	1,69	1,025	1,81	1,230	,267	,607
Ankle	1,33	,790	1,59	1,012	1,952	,166
Health	3,49	,766	3,25	,762	2,097	,151

Figure 10: Significance on the men-women comparison of pain assiduousness felt

Regarding the preference of console type and how the subjects perceived pain in different parts of their body, significance was found in the variables of wrist and hip pain, seen in Figure 11. Not playing with consoles (computer gamers) seems to increase pain in the wrist, which is much more painful compared with playing with the Xbox (p=0.013). Also not playing with consoles raises the possibilities of having hip pain, even more so if it is contrasted to those who play Wii (p=0.030) and Xbox (p=0.037) respectively. This gives us a head start for prevention intervention, due to the importance of knowing that not all devices generate the same problems.

	None (n=30)		Xbox (n=15)		Play Station (n=35)		Wii (n=13)			
Pain	Avg.	St.Dev	Avg.	St.Dev	Avg.	St.Dev	Avg.	St.Dev	F	Sig.
Head	2,37	,999	1,67	,816	2,11	,993	2,15	,899	1,789	,155
Neck	2,73	1,230	2,60	,986	2,37	1,140	2,92	1,115	,946	,422
Shoulder	2,00	1,287	1,47	,834	1,80	,964	1,85	1,144	,810	,492
Elbow	1,57	,817	1,47	,990	1,40	,736	1,31	,630	,402	,752
Wrist	2,00	,983	1,27	,594	1,74	,919	1,92	1,038	2,275	**,085**
Finger	1,37	,718	1,60	,986	1,66	1,027	1,54	,776	,594	,621
Back	3,23	1,194	2,87	1,125	2,83	1,124	2,62	1,044	1,150	,333
Hip	1,73	1,172	1,13	,516	1,51	,887	1,08	,277	2,436	**,070**
Leg	1,47	,629	1,53	,990	1,60	,847	1,23	,439	,766	,516

Knee	1,63	1,033	1,53	,990	1,97	1,272	1,54	,776	,937	,426
Ankle	1,70	1,055	1,07	,258	1,40	,847	1,23	,832	2,116	,104
Health	3,17	,699	3,73	,458	3,46	,852	3,46	,877	2,010	,118

Figure 11: Significance on the type of console used comparison of pain assiduousness felt

If exercise is considered, as noted in Figure 12, in relation to the perception of pain, significance was found in shoulder and finger pain. Gamers who do not exercise suffer from shoulder pain the most, while those who do exercise feel more pain in their fingers. There was also a significant difference in how they considered their standard health was, with those who exercise rating better than those who don't.

	Exercise (n=59)		Not exercise (n=34)			
Pain	Average	St. Dev.	Average	St. Dev.	F	Sig.
Head	2,10	,941	2,18	1,029	,127	,722
Neck	2,66	1,108	2,50	1,212	,425	,516
Shoulder	1,64	,996	2,12	1,175	4,272	**,042**
Elbow	1,42	,792	1,50	,788	,201	,655
Wrist	1,83	,874	1,68	1,036	,584	,447
Finger	1,71	1,001	1,24	,554	6,535	**,012**
Back	2,80	1,156	3,18	1,086	2,431	,122
Hip	1,46	,877	1,47	,992	,004	,948
Leg	1,46	,773	1,56	,746	,379	,540
Knee	1,73	1,142	1,74	1,024	,001	,978
Ankle	1,41	,853	1,44	,927	,033	,857
Health	3,54	,703	3,18	,834	5,094	**,026**

Figure 12: Significance on the exercise habits comparison of pain assiduousness felt

When the pain perception is weighted with visual support needs (Figure 13), it stands out that there is a statistically significant difference in headache: Those who use visual support have more headaches than those who don't. This is consistent with the high probability of having headache demonstrated by Logaraj, Madhupriya, and Hegde (Logaraj et al., 2014).

	Visual support (N=45)		No visual support (N=48)			
Pain	Average	St. Dev.	Average	St. Dev.	F	Sig.
Head	2,38	,860	1,90	1,016	6,056	**,016**
Neck	2,76	1,171	2,46	1,110	1,579	,212
Shoulder	1,98	1,158	1,67	,996	1,936	,167
Elbow	1,47	,869	1,44	,712	,032	,859
Wrist	1,87	,991	1,69	,879	,853	,358

Finger	1,49	,787	1,58	,986	,259	,612
Back	3,13	1,179	2,75	1,082	2,673	,106
Hip	1,56	1,013	1,38	,815	,902	,345
Leg	1,56	,841	1,44	,681	,557	,458
Knee	1,73	1,074	1,73	1,125	,000	,985
Ankle	1,47	,894	1,38	,866	,252	,617
Health	3,27	,809	3,54	,713	3,032	,085

Figure 13: Significance on the visual support need comparison of pain assiduousness felt

The next table, Figure 14, presents a comparison depending on the number of days a week gamers played. The only significant difference found was in hip pain: Those who play 2/3 days a week suffer more from the hip than any other time range players.

	1 day per week (n=14)		2/3 days per week (n=20)		4/5 days per week (n=19)		Daily (n=40)			
Pain	Avg.	St. Dev.	Avg.	St. Dev.	Avg.	St. Dev.	Avg.	St. Dev.	F	Sig.
Head	2,14	,663	2,10	,852	2,21	1,084	2,10	1,081	,062	,980
Neck	2,86	1,099	2,60	1,046	2,32	1,157	2,65	1,210	,645	,588
Shoul-der	1,86	1,027	2,10	1,294	1,89	1,100	1,63	,979	,911	,439
Elbow	1,50	,760	1,50	,946	1,47	,841	1,40	,709	,102	,959
Wrist	1,50	,760	2,15	1,137	1,63	,761	1,75	,927	1,674	,178
Finger	1,86	1,027	1,60	,940	1,58	,838	1,38	,838	1,093	,356
Back	3,07	1,141	3,10	1,252	2,79	1,182	2,88	1,090	,339	,797
Hip	1,21	,579	2,00	1,298	1,21	,419	1,40	,871	3,435	**,020**
Leg	1,71	,994	1,50	,761	1,53	,841	1,40	,632	,599	,618
Knee	2,00	1,301	1,75	1,070	2,00	1,202	1,50	,961	1,271	,289
Ankle	1,43	,756	1,75	1,164	1,47	,841	1,23	,733	1,665	,180
Health	3,21	,426	3,20	,834	3,53	,841	3,52	,784	1,251	,296

Figure 14: Significance on the days per week played comparison of pain assiduousness felt

We carried out another ANOVA with scores of pain while participants are playing. Depending on where they sit, compared with the pains suffered while playing, Figure 15 shows that neck, wrist, and ankle problems are significant. It was evidenced that armchair and sofa players were more likely to be affected in the neck. On the other hand, those who play in a chair usually feel pain in the wrist. The ankle problem was found significant, but not relevant because the size of the sample that answered positively to that question was too small to actually be taken in consideration.

No significance was found in comparing pain to the type of table used by the gamers. There was significance concerning how they considered their health was, but it referred to a variable that did not have enough subjects to make it valid.

Playing	Chair (n=63)		Armchair/Sofa (n=30)			
Pain	Avg.	Sta. Dev.	Avg.	Sta. Dev.	F	Sig.
Head	,30	,463	,17	,379	1,931	,168
Neck	,40	,493	,63	,490	4,692	**,033**
Shoulder	,06	,246	,13	,346	1,251	,266
Elbow	,06	,246	,07	,254	,003	,954
Wrist	,17	,383	,03	,183	3,674	**,058**
Finger	,11	,317	,10	,305	,026	,873
Back	,44	,501	,47	,507	,040	,843
Hip	,02	,126	,00	,000	,473	,493
Leg	,00	,000	,03	,183	2,126	,148
Knee	,06	,246	,07	,254	,003	,954
Ankle	,00	,000	,07	,254	4,403	**,039**
Health	3,37	,848	3,50	,572	,622	.432

Figure 15: Significance on the type of chair comparison of pain assiduousness felt

Discussion

The purpose of this study was to analyse the effects of videogames on injuries and pain. Our results provide interesting data that shows the relevance of this area for physiotherapists.

Even though the data fulfilled most of the objectives, there are some aspects that were not determined, such as the difference between the afflictions between the computer and console players or between the numbers of hours played, for either the type of mouse or keyboard used. None of these aspects were found to give any significant results. Future research could help to determine if this result is due to sample limitations or as a consequence of real absence of differences between those groups.

Hypothesis achievement and unexpected results.

From the hypotheses laid out, it could be said that we have partially confirmed them. In a global hypothesis we established that neck, shoulder, and back problems would be found. The neck and shoulder problems were found to be significant in some categories. Back problems were not found to be significant in any group, but considering the average pain perceived by the whole sample, it was clear that back pain was the most common pain felt for nearly all.

Technically speaking, the first hypothesis was not corroborated. Computer players suffered, on average, marginally more pain than console players, but it was not significant. We confirmed that console players were the ones with more neck pain and vice versa with back pain, but again, no significant results were found. This could be caused by the difference in the number of computer and console players in the sample.

On the visual issue, we found that it is true that those with vision support have more headaches than those who do not.

We also confirmed that those who play on armchair or sofa have more neck pain than those who play on chairs. In this case, there was no significance found for back pain, even though on average, sofa players had slightly more back pain than chair players.

Lastly, we found that physically active gamers feel healthier than those who are more sedentary.

The most unexpected results were mainly those that were not found. Not finding significant difference between console and computer players, the type of keyboard and mouse used, or the time spent playing, as well as not finding significance in back pain in any of the groups compared was unforeseen.

Other unexpected results related to the group where the pain was found, which was for those who play for 3-4 days per week and not for those who play more days. This is difficult to explain. It was also rare to find that for those who exercise, finger pain was significantly higher.

Main affected areas differentiating by gamer's characteristics

These are the most significantly affected areas we found throughout the variables we compared the pain answers with.

Headache: These results could be explained due to the implications of the screen exposure and bad posture of the neck in the case of headache. The use of contact lenses, and not any type of visual support, could also have something to do with this (Logaraj et al., 2014).

Hip: Pressure on the lower limbs from siting too long and different bad positions while sitting could explain hip problems. The furniture where the person sits could also be relevant. The position the hip takes depending on where one sits can compromise the joint.

Shoulder: Shoulders could have many symptomatic problems because of posture, which could be forced many times for different reasons. Because gamers spend so much time in front a computer or TV, they may have to adjust their pose several times so that they can feel comfortable, which leads to many positions that are very dangerous to the body. The keyboard and mouse can also be a cause of these problems. Even though we did not find evidence in the analysis of these variables, the possibility cannot be discarded that bad use or choice of tools can affect the shoulders of players by modifying their posture. The armrests and tables could also be a factor. Although again there was no evidence in the analysis, this should not be discarded as a possible agent due to their effect on pose. Even the stress that the games cause on the player can be reflected in their shoulders.

Shoulder symptoms have been associated with age, high screen position and shoulder elevation (Cook et al., 2000).

Shoulder pain can be prolonged by incorrect sitting posture, lasting for 3 months due to lordotic lumbo-pelvic postures (Straker et al., 2009).

Shoulder pain has also been significantly associated with emotional exhaustion (Oha et al., 2014). Shoulder pains are still believed to pose a major problem among computer office workers because of the somatization tendency and negative expected pain (Sadeghian et al., 2014).

Wrist: Lastly, wrist problems can be explained by the pressure they are exposed to while playing on the computer. Not having a correct chair could cause several poses that can force the position of the hand, making the pressure over the wrist to be too strong. These could also be caused by the keyboard and mouse selection and usage, despite the fact that the analysis did not show relevance in this matter.

Different kinds of keyboards have shown significant increase in wrist extension angle with increasing positive tilt and a large significant decrease in wrist extension with negative tilt, for example an AS keyboard compared with a standard flat keyboard. There is evidence that there is a moderate significant decrease in wrist extension angle with an FA keyboard compared with a standard keyboard. It is also known that there is a small non-significant decrease in wrist extension with an AT keyboard compared with a standard flat keyboard (Baker & Cidboy, 2006).

Wrist and hand symptoms have been demonstrated to have as major risks factors stress and shoulder elevation (Cook et al., 2000).

Wrist pain has also been associated with older age, lower odds of left-handedness or ambidexterity, belief that musculoskeletal problems are currently caused by work, and time pressures at work (Villanueva et al., 1997).

Other results given point towards to neck and finger pain with minor notoriety.

Neck: Because of where the neck pain was found to be more common, it could be thought that forced posture by sitting in poorly ergonomically designed furniture such as an armchair or a sofa while playing with video games, regardless of if it is on computer or console, could be the cause.

Related to the examination of the relationship between computer mouse use and musculoskeletal symptoms in the neck, shoulder, wrist or hand, and upper back, no relationship has been found between hours of mouse use per day and symptoms. A relationship between the mouse-specific variable of arm abduction and musculoskeletal symptoms in the neck was found in addition to relationships between non-mouse-specific risk factors. It has been noted that stress, screen height, and shoulder elevation; risk factors previously associated with keyboard use, are also risk factors for mouse users. Neck symptoms have been associated with low or high screen height. Time with the hand positioned on the mouse has been associated to neck symptoms when considered in univariate analysis but not when combined with other significant factors via logistic regression. All of this concludes that mouse use may contribute to neck discomfort (Cook et al., 2000).

There is evidence that neck pain can be prolonged with an incorrect sitting posture, lasting for 3 months. Prolonged neck pain has been associated with more lordotic lumbo-pelvic postures (Straker et al., 2009). A high prevalence of musculoskeletal pain, especially in the neck and lower back, among computer users has been found. Neck pain has been found to be significantly more common in women at older ages and with somatising tendency and belief that musculoskeletal problems are commonly caused by work (Oha, 2014).

There is evidence that neck pain still poses a major problem among computer office workers and somatisation tendency and negative expected pain (Sadeghian et al., 2014).

Research centred on the sitting posture has established that a relatively upright posture results from an increase in the vertical location of the screen. This is manifested by the strong significant correlation between neck flexion and neck extensor muscle activity seen when changing the height of the screen (Villanueva et al., 1997).

A series of experiments has been made to investigate the mechanisms of efficacy of cervical muscle retraining in prolonged sitting computer users, using exercises to train the craniocervical flexor muscles, or an endure-strength training regimen for the cervical flexor muscles which demonstrated that an exercise program targeted at retraining the craniocervical flexor muscles improved the ability to maintain a neutral cervical posture during prolonged sitting (Falla et al., 2007).

Finger: Finger pain was unexpectedly found significant only in those players who are used to doing physical activity. The only reason that could explain this fact is that maybe these subjects may play less than those who don't exercise, and because of this, they would be less used to typing, clicking, and using console controllers, which could justify their perception of finger pain.

Utility

This research paper is one of the first steps to contribute to understanding the way eSports players interact with their environmental conditions, such as personal conditions, furniture, gaming tools, health habits, or time spent playing. It also gives a first view of global pains that gamers feel normally and while playing. The goal of this study was to be able to fill in the blanks concerning the health and primary risks of eSports players, so that in the future patients that could arise from the exercise of this sport won't be strangers to us. The data of this research may be illustrative and help to develop prevention and treatment programs for gamers' injuries. This study, as other research before, shows that an ergonomic approach is more than justified for gamers, especially the eSports athletes.

In this sense, it is possible to apply well-documented techniques to these emerging patients.

Combined with other research, this paper could help set the basis for new approaches to prevent ailments. For example, a comparison of changes in objectively measured workplace sitting time following a multi-component intervention, based on a "stand up, sit less, move more" educational program with a height-adjustable workstations versus the installation of height-adjustable workstations alone that resulted in a reduction of office workers' sitting time during work hours relative to the provision of height-adjustable workstations alone, which concluded that multi-component programs targeting workplace sitting may achieve more substantial reductions in office workers' sitting time (Neuhaus et al., 2014). Physiotherapists could use both of these studies to make use of the health education training they have and create a prevention program.

Other articles suggest a comparison of the effectiveness of two exercises in stretching the hamstring muscle: the passive straight leg raise exercise, and knee extension in sitting, an exercise in which the knee joint is passively extended in the sitting position, which concluded that both exercises were effective at improving forward bending, and the angles of active straight leg raise and knee joint extension, knee extension in sitting being more widely used because it can be done more easily (Jang et al., 2013). If back problems are most common in gamers, this exercise could be implanted in a prevention program as well. Also a self-modelling training method, using webcam photos, has been laid out. This was presented on the workers' computer screens in order to improve their workplace posture, comparing a photo-training intervention with a conventional office ergonomic intervention group, and with a control group to evaluate their effectiveness in reducing musculoskeletal risk, both between genders and over time. The intervention given to the office ergonomic training group by an ergonomist included two aspects: 1) personal training on how to improve their posture while working on the computer 2) practical instruction on how to modify their workstation. The self-modelling photo-training group received the office ergonomic training as detailed above and in addition also received self-modelling photo-training feedback. After receiving the office ergonomic training, the participant was asked to sit correctly according to the training. The ergonomist verified that this posture was the optimal working posture. A photograph of this correct posture was taken using the webcam. It proved that it was effective for improving sitting posture of workers at computer work stations (Taieb-Maimon et al., 2012). This research shows the importance of new and innovative methods for postural health. We can come up with an interactive method to remind gamers while playing to maintain their posture upright.

Limitations and future studies

While trying to cover such a large number of fields, very small groups were obtained, and that fact does not allow us to generalize the results. It would have been interesting to have a larger sample of players who played 6 days a week for at least 8 hours a day, so that we could compare results to actual eSports athletes.

Once this study is reviewed, many specific studies can be followed from here. For instance, from each variable item we asked in the survey, there could be a specific study.

Age, gender, and employment should be more thoroughly studied, even more so if studying eSports players. In this direction, time spent and type of device used should be looked into as well for eSports players. Clinical trials should be used to identify the specifics of which injuries are more common and how the furniture and accessories they use affect their health. Digging deeper in this aspect could help even more to prevent many problems that could appear in a very short period of time.

Using the technology shown in a psychometric testing description of a new three-dimensional (3D), portable, non-invasive posture analysis tool which was first tried in Mannequin and then in high school students in a sitting posture, and that demonstrated to be valid and reliable could also be found to be useful to help to narrow even more the postural habits of videogame players (Brink et al., 2013).

Following the previous line of posture research, taking the model of a description of the variability of five postural angles in a cohort of asymptomatic high school students whilst working on desktop computers, in a typical South African school computer classroom placing two 3D-PAT camera units on each side of the student, facing the lateral aspect of the student, calibrated using a pyramid calibration object prior to each data capture. They discovered that angles producing movement in the sagittal plane were both individually or in combination associated with height, weight, and body mass index, where trunk flexion was found to be the most variable postural angle measured and increased neck flexion was significantly associated with increased weight (Brink et al., 2014). This information should also be pursued regarding videogame players, which could open a whole new line of investigation and give more information of the postural habits of gamers in order to find ways to ensure their health.

An observational study or a clinical trial focused on those specific aspects could clarify better which are the most relevant injuries and how to avoid them. Also digging deeper in any other aspect of this initial study of the gaming community could be interesting to try and verify the results on this research.

Conclusions

The study has shown that there is still much to investigate regarding videogame players. After all, there are mo[re]
questions than answers throughout this research. It has been established that there are more male than fema[le]
players. There are more computer players than console ones. There is a notable amount of players with back pa[in]
compared to any other ailment. In term of significance between groups, head, shoulder, hip, and wrist proble[m]
seem to be the most important. Neck and finger ailments appear to be also substantial, but in less magnitu[de]
Gender, type of console, exercise habits, visual support, days per week played, and type of seat have shown to [be]
the most important aspects related to the health of the gaming community.

The importance of this study lies in the novelty of it. There are no specific researches on this particular subje[ct]
meaning this could be a ground-breaking investigation that could lead to many more. It will be useful for ma[ny]
health experts who will probably need information about the growing gamer community, especially in the preve[n-]
tion sector. Here is where most of the relevance of this inquiry is, the importance of knowing the most comm[on]
physical problems and in which groups they can be found is crucial to prepare prevention protocols and to crea[te]
more ergonomic items. It will also allow finding the source of many injuries to treat them properly.

Christian Martin ic currently working as junior orthopedic physiotherapist at the BMI Ross Hall Hospital [in]
Scotland. He has a diploma as a pathologic lab technician and graduated as physio from La Universidad de [La]
Laguna in Tenerife.

References

Baker, N., Cidboy, E. (2006). The Effect of Three Alternative Keyboard Designs on Forearm Pronation, Wrist Extension, and Ulnar Deviation: A Meta-Analysis. American Journal of Occupational Therapy, 60(1), 40-49.

Bener, A., Dafeeah, E., Alnaqbi, K. (2014). Prevalence and Correlates of Low Back Pain in Primary Care: What Are the Contributing Factors in a Rapidly Developing Country?. Asian Spine J, 8(3), 227-236.

Brink, Y., Louw, Q., Grimmer, K., Jordaan, E. (2014). The spinal posture of computing adolescents in a real-life setting. BMC Musculoskeletal Disorders, 15(1), 212-221.

Brink, Y., Louw, Q., Grimmer, K., Schreve, K., Van Der Westhuizen, G., Jordaan, E. (2013). Development of a cost effective three-dimensional posture analysis tool: validity and reliability. BMC Musculoskeletal Disorders, 14(1), 335-145.

Cañas, J. J., Waerns, Y. (2001). Ergonomía Cognitiva: Aspectos Psicológicos de la interacción de las personas con la tecnología de la información. Madrid: Editorial Médica Panamericana.

Chau, J., Daley, M., Dunn, S., Srinivasan, A., Do, A., Bauman, A. (2014). The effectiveness of sit-stand workstations for changing office workers' sitting time: results from the Stand@Work randomized controlled trial pilot. Int J Behav. Nutr. Phys. Act, 11(1), 1-10.

Cook, C., Burgess-Limerick, R., Chang, S. (2000). The prevalence of neck and upper extremity musculoskeletal symptoms in computer mouse users. International Journal of Industrial Ergonomics, 26(3), 347-356.

De Wall, M., Van Riel, M. P. J. M., Snijders, C. J. (1992). The effect on sitting posture of a desk with a 10° inclination for reading and writing. Applied Ergonomics, 23(3), 575-584.

Defloor, T., Grypdonck, M. (1999). Sitting posture and prevention of pressure ulcers. Applied Nursing Research, 12(3), 136-142.

Dutta, N., Koepp, G., Stovitz, S., Levine, J., Pereira, M. (2014). Using Sit-Stand Workstations to Decrease Sedentary Time in Office Workers: A Randomized Crossover Trial. IJERPH, 11(7), 6653-6665.

Falla, D., Jull, G., Russell, T., Vicenzino, B., Hodges, P. (2007). Effect of Neck Exercise on Sitting Posture in Patients with Chronic Neck Pain. Physical Therapy, 87(4), 408-417.

forbes.com. (2015, April 12). Riot's 'League of Legends' Reveals Astonishing 27 Million Daily Players, 67 Million Monthly. Retrieved from http://www.forbes.com/sites/insertcoin/2014/01/27/riots-league-of-legends-reveals-astonishing-27-million-daily-players-67-million-monthly/

forbes.com. (2015, April 12). Second US College Now Offering League of Legends Scholarship. Retrieved from http://www.forbes.com/sites/insertcoin/2015/01/08/second-us-college-now-offering-league-of-legends-scholarship/

forbes.com. (2015, April 12). The US Now Recognizes eSports Players as Professional Athletes. Retrieved from http://www.forbes.com/sites/insertcoin/2013/07/14/the-u-s-now-recognizes-eSports-players-as-professional-athletes/

Frey, J., Tecklin, J. (1986). Comparison of lumbar curves when sitting on the Westnofa Balans® multi-chair, sitting on a conventional chair, and standing. Physical Therapy, 66(9), 1365-1369.

González-Gross, M., Meléndez, A. (2013). Sedentarism, active lifestyle and sport: impact on health and obesity prevention. Nutrición Hospitalaria, 28(5), 89-98.

Grondin, D., Triano, J., Tran, S., Soave, D. (2013). The effect of a lumbar support pillow on lumbar posture and comfort during a prolonged seated task. Chiropr Man Therap, 21(1), 21-30.

Helajärvi, H., Rosenström, T., Pahkala, K., Kähönen, M., Lehtimäki, T., Heinonen, O. (2014). Exploring Causality between TV Viewing and Weight Change in Young and Middle-Aged Adults. The Cardiovascular Risk in Young Finns Study. PLoS ONE, 9(7), 1-11.

Jang, J., Koh, E., Han, D. (2013). The Effectiveness of Passive Knee Extension Exercise in the Sitting Position on Stretching of the Hamstring Muscles of Patients with Lower Back Pain. Journal of Physical Therapy Science, 25(4), 501-504.

Ketola, R., Toivonen, R., Häkkänen, M., Luukkonen, R., Takala, E., Viikari-Juntura, E. (2002). Effects of ergonomic intervention in work with video display units. Scand J Work Environ Health, 28(1), 18-24.

Kim, M., Yoo, W. (2013). Comparison of the Hamstring Muscle Activity and Flexion-Relaxation Ratio between Asymptomatic Persons and Computer Work-related Low Back Pain Sufferers. Journal of Physical Therapy Science, 25(5), 535-536.

Kryger, A. (2003). Does computer use pose an occupational hazard for forearm pain; from the NUDATA study? Occupational and Environmental Medicine, 60(11), 14-23.

Lis, A., Black, K., Korn, H., Nordin, M. (2016). Association between sitting and occupational LBP. European Spine Journal, 16(2), 283-298.

Logaraj. M., Madhupriya, V., Hegde, S. (2014). Computer vision syndrome and associated factors among medical and engineering students in Chennai. Ann Med Health Sci Res, 4(2), 179–185.

M-Pranesh, A., Rakheja, S., Demont, R. (2010). Influence of Support Conditions on Vertical Whole-body Vibration of the Seated Human Body. Industrial Health, 48(5), 682-697.

Neuhaus, M., Healy, G., Dunstan, D., Owen, N., EakIN, E. (2014). Workplace Sitting and Height-Adjustable Workstations. American Journal of Preventive Medicine, 46(1), 30-40.

O'Sullivan, P., Dankaerts, W., Burnett, A., Farrell, G., Jefford, E., Naylor, C. (2006). Effect of Different Upright Sitting Postures on Spinal-Pelvic Curvature and Trunk Muscle Activation in a Pain-Free Population. Spine, 31(19), 707-712.

Occhipinti E., Colombini, D. (1986). Sitting posture:

Analysis of lumbar stresses with upper limbs supported. Applied Ergonomics, 17(4), 1333-1346.

Oham, K., Animägi, L., Pääsuke, M., Coggon, D., Merisalu, E. (2014). Individual and work-related risk factors for musculoskeletal pain: a cross-sectional study among Estonian computer users. BMC Musculoskeletal Disorders, 15(1), 181-186.

Park, W., Kim, Y., Lee, T., Sung, P. (2012). Factors affecting shoulder–pelvic integration during axial trunk rotation in subjects with recurrent low back pain. European Spine Journal, 21(7), 1316-1323.

pcgamer.com. (2015, April 12). Valve explains how CS:GO became the second most-played game on Steam. Retrieved from http://www.pcgamer.com/valve-explains-how-csgo-became-the-second-most-played-game-on-steam/

Ringseis, R., Eder, K., Mooren, F., Krüger, K. (2015). Metabolic signals and innate immune activation in obesity and exercise. Inflammation, 10(14), 157-167.

Sadeghian, F., Raei, M., Amiri, M. (2014). Persistent of Neck/Shoulder Pain among Computer Office Workers with Specific Attention to Pain Expectation, Somatization Tendency, and Beliefs. International Journal of Preventive Medicine, 5(9), 1169–1177.

Shephard, R. (2012). Physical activity levels, ownership of goods promoting sedentary behavior and risk of myocardial infarction: results of the INTERHEART study. Yearbook of Sports Medicine, 167-168.

Sparks, D., Chase, D., Coughlin, L. (2009). Wii have a problem: a review of self-reported Wii related injuries. Informatics in primary care, 17(1), 55-57.

Statista.com. (2015, April 12). Total Number of Game Consoles sold worldwide by Console Type. Retrieved from http://www.statista.com/statistics/268966/total-number-of-game-consoles-sold-worldwide-by-console-type/

Straker, L., O'sullivan, P., Smith, A., Perry, M. (2009). Relationships between prolonged neck/shoulder pain and sitting spinal posture in male and female adolescents. Manual Therapy, 14(3), 321-329.

Taieb-Maimon, M., Cwikel, J., Shapira, B., Orenstein, I. (2012). The effectiveness of a training method using self-modeling webcam photos for reducing musculoskeletal risk among office workers using computers. Applied Ergonomics, 43(2), 376-385.

Theesa.com. (2015, April 12). Essential Facts about the Computer Industry. Retrieved from http://www.theesa.com/wp-content/uploads/2014/10/ESA_EF_2014.pdf

Van Deursen, L., Patijn, J., Durinck, J. (1999). Sitting and low back pain: the positive effect of rotatory dynamic stimuli during prolonged sitting. European Spine Journal, 8(3), 187-193.

Villanueva, M., Jonai, H., Sotoyama, M., Hisanaga, N., Takeuchi, Y., Saito, S. (1997). Sitting Posture and Neck and Shoulder Muscle Activities at Different Screen Height Settings of the Visual Display Terminal. INDUSTRIAL HEALTH, 35(3), 330-336.

Voerman, G., Sandsjö, L., Vollenbroek-Hutten, M., Larsman, P., Kadefors, R., Hermens, H. (2007). Effects of

Ambulant Myofeedback Training and Ergonomic Coun-selling in Female Computer Workers with Work-Related Neck-Shoulder Complaints: A Randomized Controlled Trial. J Occup Rehabil, 17(1), 137-152.

Wang, X. (1999). A behavior-based inverse kinematics algo-rithm to predict arm prehension postures for computer-aided ergonomic evaluation. Journal of Biomechanics, 32(5), 453-460.

Zemp, R., Taylor, W., Lorenzetti, S. (2013). In Vivo Spinal Posture during Upright and Reclined Sitting in an Office Chair. BioMed Research International, 1-5.

Lightning Source UK Ltd.
Milton Keynes UK
UKHW031014180619

344611UK00008B/204/P